Commu
With Myself:
A Journal

Communicating With Myself: A Journal

Second Edition

Jacquelyn B. Carr

WCB Wm. C. Brown Publishers

Book Team

Editor *Stan Stoga*
Production Editor *Carla D. Arnold*

WCB Wm. C. Brown Publishers

President *G. Franklin Lewis*
Vice President, Publisher *George Wm. Bergquist*
Vice President, Publisher *Thomas E. Doran*
Vice President, Operations and Production *Beverly Kolz*
National Sales Manager *Virginia S. Moffat*
Senior Marketing Manager *Kathy Law Laube*
Marketing Manager *Kathleen Nietzke*
Executive Editor *Edgar J. Laube*
Managing Editor, Production *Colleen A. Yonda*
Production Editorial Manager *Julie A. Kennedy*
Production Editorial Manager *Ann Fuerste*
Publishing Services Manager *Karen J. Slaght*
Manager of Visuals and Design *Faye M. Schilling*

Cover design by Benoit & Associates

Cover image from COMSTOCK, Inc./Michael Stuckey

Copyright © 1979 by The Benjamin/Cummings Publishing Company, Inc. Philippines copyright 1979 by The Benjamin/Cummings Publishing Company, Inc.

Copyright © 1984, 1991 by Wm. C. Brown Publishers. All rights reserved

Library of Congress Catalog Card Number: 89-82704

ISBN 0-697-11518-6

No part of this publication may be reproduced, stored in a retrieval system, or transmitted, in any form or by any means, electronic, mechanical, photocopying, recording, or otherwise, without the prior written permission of the publisher.

Printed in the United States of America by Wm. C. Brown Publishers, 2460 Kerper Boulevard, Dubuque, IA 52001

10 9 8

The charm of the journal must consist in a certain greenness . . . and not in maturity. Here I cannot afford to be remembering what I said or did . . . but what I am and aspire to become.

Henry David Thoreau

Contents

To the Reader   xi

PART ONE   **CREATING MEANING**   1

Chapter 1: The Journal   3
What Is a Journal?   4
Why Do People Write Journals?   4
    Journals as History   5
    Journals as Autobiography   6
    Journals as Creative Writing   6
    Journals as Self-Exploration   7
Keeping a Journal   8
Organizing a Journal   10
Rereading Your Journal   12

Chapter 2: Perception and Context   15
Sensory Receptors   16
Experience   17
Interpretation   18
Exploring Perception   19
    Conflicting Perceptions   20
    Changing Perceptions   22

Exploring Context 23
   Culture as Context 24
   Awareness of Context 26

Chapter 3: Creating Self-Concept 29

Your Historical Past 30
   Family Memories 30
   Childhood Memories 34
The Present 40
   Self-Image 40
   Self-Esteem 49
   Multiple Selves 53

Chapter 4: Transformation and Change 57

Personal Values 61
   Values and Time 62
   Values and Money 65
   Values in Transition 68
   Decision-Making 70
   Marking Transitions 78

PART TWO ASPECTS OF COMMUNICATION 81

Chapter 5: How the Body Communicates 83

Nonverbal Communication 84
Rules about Touching 89
Body Work 91

Chapter 6: How Feelings Communicate 95

Programmed Emotional Responses 96
Ambivalence and Conflict 105
Hidden Feelings 107
Emotional Style 109
Owning Your Feelings 110

Chapter 7: How Language Communicates 111

Watching Your Language 112
The Language of "Right" and "Wrong" 117
The Limits of Language 119

Chapter 8: How the Mind Communicates 123

Justifying and Rationalizing 127
Contemplation 129
Mind Potential 129
The Split Mind 130
Meditation 132
Recording Your Dreams 133
Types of Imagination 133
    Reproductive Imagination 134
    Creative Imagination 135
    Guided Imagery 135
New Directions 137

Chapter 9: How Actions Communicate 139

Interpersonal Needs 140
Roles We Play 142
    Parent Roles 145
    How to Parent the Child Inside 150
Changing Behavior 152

PART THREE   COMMUNICATING WITH OTHERS 157

Chapter 10: Communicating in Relationships 159

Relationship Skills 160
Personality Differences 161
Social Expectations 164
Kinds of Relationships 165
    Friendship 166
    Support Networks 173
    Communicating at Work 173
    Intimate Relationships 176
Love 177
Ending Relationships 183

Chapter 11: Communication Barriers   187

Checklist of Communication Problems   188
Attitude   188
Self-Deception   189
Defense Mechanisms   190
Conflict Resolution   192
The Double Bind   193
Evaluating Your Communication Skills   194

Chapter 12: The Search for a Way of Life   201

Ethical Dilemmas   204
   Personal Ethics   205
   Agreements   207
Ethics and Choice   208
   Choosing a World View   209
   Integrity   210
Common Ground   210
Creating a Home   211
The Journey   212

To The Reader

> *The unexamined life is not worth living.*
> *Plato*

Each of us has an outer and an inner existence—a social and a personal life. We often get so caught up in the daily processes of living that the inner self gets lost. The second edition of *Communicating with Myself: A Journal* presents you with an opportunity to explore the core of yourself and unite the many aspects of you that hide behind the trees in the forest. This book contains a wealth of exploratory ways to reconnect those parts that are hidden from consciousness. Uncovering constantly changing values and beliefs—only two important aspects—and examining them can be a spiritual awakening that can lead you to discover unknown qualities and to find more productive directions for your life.

This journal contains such a wealth of thought-provoking subjects that it will take a lifetime to explore them all. You set your pace—weeks, months, or years—and you choose your depth—lightly touching the surface or going deeper and deeper into the source. In your journal, you can create a dependable, loving friend who will stand by and support you to replace the critic who often belittles you. This friend with whom you carry on a dialogue in your thoughts will be with you, either consciously or unconsciously, for your entire life.

The personal journal is cumulative, always there whether you write once a day, week, month or year. You will grow increasingly comfortable with this journal guide as you learn unique ways to research your inner world with all of its potentially rich resources. This book offers ways to establish deep, inner dialogues with the self and some helpful approaches to experiencing resources present in memories, daydreams, and fantasies.

Trust yourself to find the most effective and productive ways to use the journal, personal ways that can be continuously redesigned. Some suggestions can be followed simply by reflecting on what you read, others by jotting down thoughts. Although some readers would prefer large, blank spaces for writing in the text, most readers want more thought-provoking exercises that require space for continual development. Separate, blank pages inserted into a loose leaf notebook allow you to add future thoughts reflecting personal transitions and individual growth.

You are the architect and designer of your personal journal. It can be used to record and reflect upon daily activities—to explore values, define goals, make decisions, and set agendas for actions that will move you in the directions you wish to go. Your journal can help you clarify many of the influences that affect relationships in your life. It allows your imagination to roam and your creativity to expand as you select subjects that fit your personal modes of thinking and feeling. As you notice how your past, present, and future run like a thread through your life, you will become aware that you are *always* in transition.

Memories, sense impressions, interior monologues—all lead beyond themselves to emotional responses or mental associations involving yourself and others. The journal process will reward you with potentially astonishing breakthroughs as you move through dark tunnels into the light. The greatest value of your journal is to discover new paths toward the full development of your potential as a human being.

Part One

Creating Meaning

> We must learn to reawaken and keep ourselves awake . . . by an infinite expectation of the dawn.
>
> Thoreau

Each of the twelve chapters in this journal is a small unit. These units are divided into three parts. In Part 1, *Creating Meaning,* Chapter 1 defines the journal and how you can use it to find personal meaning in your life and in the world. Chapter 2 gives you an opportunity to explore your personal perceptions of yourself, others, and your world in the context in which you live. Chapter 3 includes a study of your life, your historical past, and your self-image. Chapter 4 explores personal values and goals in the transformation process.

We assume all too readily that observations come naturally, like breathing. The result is that many of us live in a world whose parameters are the size of a small closet. We become familiar with a few things and lock into a very limited vision of what life is all about. Although there will always be untapped wells of awareness, these four chapters in Part 1 give you a foundation upon which to expand your consciousness of yourself in the context of your life.

The value of keeping a journal is that we remember our best hours and stimulate ourselves.

Thoreau

1

The Journal

Language is a medium through which we encounter the world and establish our relationship with it. It enables us to discover, interpret, and communicate our experiences. Thus words become the primary content of our lives; they literally shape our concepts of reality.

When humans learned to read and write, they began to record their thoughts and experiences. Writing, an important form of expressing and extending the self in language, is a complex and demanding process. It never results in presenting the whole self, for each of us has many selves. To further complicate our attempts to capture it, the self is always in transition, continuously changing. Through writing, we become more conscious of our inner thoughts, emotional responses, and experiences. When we put words into a concrete, written form, we capture the essence of a life and experience the miracles of self-discovery through self-expression.

WHAT IS A JOURNAL?

> *No man remains quite what he was when he recognizes himself.*
> Thomas Mann

Each of us has a complex and continuous interior language, a constantly flowing stream of words, phrases, images, and ideas—an internal monologue, a stream of consciousness that needs no direction to shape it into writing. *A journal is a personal notebook that attempts to capture this constant internal flow.* A journal differs from a diary, which is a daily written account of activities, yet a journal can include a diary. A journal also differs from an autobiography, which is the story of a person's life written by that person, yet a journal is often used as the foundation for an autobiography.

A journal, like a self-adjusting compass, can guide you in seeking direction for your life. Regardless of age, social background, or education, a journal enables you to begin wherever you are and move at your own tempo, recording whatever goes through your mind. It is an instrument that can be used in privacy, giving its writer a wealth of feedback to crystallize decisions and help create meaning in life. At times an exciting awareness breaks through like the dawn of a new day. The journal records this insight as part of a continuous process, as the writer reconstructs the past, records the present, and imagines the future. At a later date, rereading journal entries helps the writer to discover personal growth and evolution.

The journal can also strengthen inner capacities as the writer recognizes his or her own identity. Like a thread of movement, inner resources unfold and reveal themselves as the writer records what has just been recognized. Writing takes the impulse of the moment, gives it form, makes it permanent. *Ultimately the journal is a relationship with the self.*

WHY DO PEOPLE WRITE JOURNALS?

> *So long as man is capable of self-renewal, he is a living being.*
> Henri Frederic Amiel

When you keep a journal you make a gift of your past to your future. You are creating your own history. A journal records your inner life and its developments. Outer events may be recorded inasmuch as they relate to inner events (feelings and thoughts), but the focus is on the unfolding awareness of the self in the world—on the new meanings, values, and interrelationships as you discover them. If, at times, you choose to share appropriate parts of your journal with those you love, you give them a gift of yourself.

The journal is one of the most useful instruments we have for long-term self-development. It contains personal experiences and records what a person sees, feels, and thinks. Something above and beyond ordinary communication takes place when you record the movement of your life. You learn to be more articulate about your beliefs and experiences. When you clarify them, you change your perceptions and expand your horizons. The feedback from the journal is cumulative and can be a primary source of your own autobiography.

In your journal, write a few goals for personal growth.
"I want . . ."

- To be more aware of my body, feelings, thoughts, actions and their interactions
- To be more aware of how I use language; to be more precise with words and how I put them together
- To be more aware of my self-concept and to notice changes in how I project myself in different situations
- To increase feelings of self-worth in both myself and others
- To expand my consciousness by focusing on dreams, imagery, myths, and intuition
- To notice how others communicate nonverbally (with their body, facial expressions, tone of voice, etc.)
- To be able to listen to both verbal and nonverbal language
- To learn more about intimacy, trust, and risk in relationships
- To become more sensitive to the feelings of others
- To help establish a sense of community in my family and in other life situations
- To create a sense of purpose in my life and to develop some guidelines for moving toward that purpose

Occasionally reread what you have written so that you can check your progress or change directions.

Journals as History

Individuals have kept records of their personal lives from the beginning of written history. These diaries, letters, notebooks, and journals provide us with information about writers, actors, scientists, philosophers, and political leaders in other times and places. The most famous early journal was kept by Samuel Pepys, an Englishman who began his diaries on January 1, 1660. Samuel Sewall, an American, began his diaries as a young man in 1674. For 55 years, he wrote journals recording his personal and public life in the colonies.

Many American women who migrated to the West between 1840 and 1870 wrote letters and journals describing their experiences crossing the country before the western states were formed. These writings, which were collected and published in 1982 by Lillian Schlissel in *Women's Diaries of the Westward Journey,* tell the stories of ordinary women as they traveled across the wilderness.

Journals as Autobiography

"I write my life's story because my great grandmother who was born in a covered wagon in 1853 didn't. My parents didn't write either. There's an emptiness inside me they could have filled. I write to fill that emptiness both for myself and for my own grandchildren."

Anonymous

No matter how insignificant it might appear on the surface, every life is worth recording. The inner individual life is rich in fantasy, emotion, and dreams. Like a mirror, each life reflects a historical time and place. A century ago, some of our ancestors didn't read or write. But future generations will cherish our letters, historical documents, and written records. We write journals first for ourselves and then for the benefit of future generations.

Journals as Creative Writing

Most of us at one time or another think: "Some day I'll write a story." But in school, we found writing more complicated than reading. Although we learned to read, we spent less time writing. When teachers assigned writing, we were marked down for mechanical and grammatical errors. Instead of interpreting these corrections as help, some of us became discouraged and avoided writing altogether.

Journal writing does not require correct spelling or grammar. It's not the structure or mechanics but the *content* of what you write in a journal that will help you expand your self-awareness and develop your creativity.

Some people find it as difficult to start and keep up a journal as it is to start and keep up a regular physical exercise program. But if once every six months or even once a year you write in a journal, you have a permanent record that won't get flabby without use. If you write in a journal once a week, it is like training for a race. At first it may seem awkward. Then a point comes when you break through "the wall" and start running on automatic. Writing is to the mind what exercise is to the body. Writing improves your language skills which in turn brings a sense of satisfaction.

Of all written forms, diaries and journals are the closest to speech. Journal writers quickly jot down feelings, thoughts, and actions of a particular time and place. Their stories lack formality. Yet the personality of the writer comes through in choice of content, the balance of description to action, the emphasis on things or people. Some writers use their journals for play. Like children, they explore and experiment with new interests using different stylistic forms such as short stories, essays, and poetry.

Many published writers begin their apprenticeship with notebooks and journals in which they develop the habit of writing. From these writings, they find source material for manuscripts that eventually find their way into print. Each of us, through journal writing, can be a creative writer.

Journals as Self-Exploration

> *What a piece of work is a man!*
> *How noble in reason!*
> *How infinite in faculty!*
> *William Shakespeare*

Of the many ways to use journals, one of the most common is to use them for self-study—to expand self-awareness, to define self-identity, and to build self-esteem. You can begin by exploring your family history.

Stop reading, pick up a pen, and on lined paper jot down responses to the following. Just let your mind run on and write as fast as you can without stopping.

- Begin with, "I was born . . ."
- Write your first memories: "When I was five . . ."
- Write about your grandparents: "My mother's father . . ."
- Write about your parents: "My dad . . ."
- Write about a teacher: "My favorite teacher . . ."
- Explore the present:
    1. Here and now—Who am I?
    2. What is happening in my life?
    3. What is important to me?
    4. What do I want?
    5. What do I have to do to get what I want?
    6. What is in the way of my getting what I want?
    7. How can I start doing it?

Self-exploration is not the same as self-absorption. Although life begins with the self, it does not end there. Exclusive focusing on selfish interests leads to emptiness. However, self-intimacy is the bedrock for intimacy with others. We can form better relationships if we know who we are. Ultimately, each of us wants to find a purpose in life. For many, our goals include making a contribution to our world.

People who know who they are, what they want, what their natural aptitudes are, how to capitalize on their strengths and how to compensate for their weaknesses have a special kind of intelligence. They know how to make their lives work. *Journals increase a writer's introspective intelligence—which is the gift of self-understanding.*

What do you want to gain by keeping a journal? The journal:

- Creates an opportunity for self-study by clarifying perception and expanding awareness
- Results in more accurate thinking and expression
- Records differences between real responses as opposed to programmed or habitual responses
- Shows the writer that his/her view of the world is unique
- Demonstrates through experience that creativity resides in the individual writer
- Encourages the writer to look for something new every day
- Compensates for a faulty memory and provides a vehicle for looking back to see one's personal growth and change
- Provides an opportunity to clarify values and goals and order priorities
- Increases powers of observation and description as well as powers of reflection
- Creates a feeling of wholeness through an experience of continuity and coherence
- Provides a permanent, concrete record of thoughts and feelings
- Exposes internal conflicts and ambivalent feelings
- Helps to define problems and reduce confusion
- Provides an opportunity to express powerful and disruptive emotions that otherwise might remain bottled up inside
- Offers a safe place to be authentic and real

Select two items from this list. Check them every once in a while to see if you are moving in the directions you want.

KEEPING A JOURNAL

Although this edition of *Communicating with Myself: A Journal* makes many suggestions throughout the book about subjects for writing, you are the author of your journal. You are the one who decides when to write, what to write about, what to say, and how to say it. You are writing notes to yourself about what matters to you. You are free to write *anything,* at any time, in any form. If you want ideas, you can turn the pages of this book and let your mind wander until you find something that catches your interest.

Experienced journal writers use certain techniques. For example, some carry a little notebook. They jot down words or thoughts the minute they occur. Others use paper on which they can capture the force and flow of larger paragraphs when something happens. Most journal writers find it helpful to establish a regular time for writing in their journals. Those who want daily records can usually remember what happened yesterday, and with the help of a pocket calendar, they can write every other day.

For those less concerned about the details of daily routines, a time set aside on a particular day once a week can capture the most important thoughts and feelings of the last seven days. They might want to capture special occasions—birthdays, graduations, wedding anniversaries; or holidays—Easter, Mother's Day, Thanksgiving. Yearly letters mailed with Christmas cards summarize some highlights of the past year.

If you can't think of anything to say, write anyway. Start with, "I'm blocking. I can't think of anything to write. My block feels like . . .". Or look around the room. Find an object that reminds you of something. Look out the window . . . find some stimulus outside yourself to start a response. Or use a picture album, an old scrapbook, an old letter or postcard. The want ads in the newspaper, an article or an interview on T.V., or the news—any one of these may trigger a response. Go back through your journal and find an entry that brings out a response. If you are preoccupied with a problem, describe it. Think of some alternative courses of action. Make a list for or against the different solutions.

Although routines and habits help many of us, not everyone wants a well-regulated life. If you write one page a week, you will have a fifty page journal covering a year in your life. Some years you will write less and other years more. What you write and how often you write is your free choice. There are no rules or requirements, and therefore no reason for guilt. In addition to free self-expression, the primary goal is to enjoy your journal.

The Writing Situation—These suggestions may be useful:

- Use a binder or loose-leaf notebook so that you can add something you forgot or expand on something you left unfinished. Later, you may want to reorganize your entries.

- Write using whatever methods or materials are most comfortable for you: pen, dark pencil, typewriter, or word processor.

- Mark down the date of each entry for future reference, for continuity, or for a developmental perspective.

- Write on one side of the paper. You may want to add words, passages, quotes, drawings, photos, or articles on the opposite page.

- Write on a subject until you have said all that you want to say whether it be in a few words or in ten pages. There are no minimum or maximum numbers of words.

- Develop the ability to describe rather than to judge yourself or others.
- Be aware of when you are analyzing or interpreting, justifying or rationalizing.
- Use the personal point of view (I, me, mine). This is the story of your life. The first person point of view is most appropriate.
- Write freely. Notice if you are censoring or distorting your real feelings or thoughts. Do not worry about finding just the "right" words. Spelling, punctuation, and grammar are not the focus of journal writing.
- Set aside what you have written. At a later date, when you reread what you have written, be aware of your feelings and thoughts. Your responses to your journal will often provide material for future entries.
- Use scissors and scotch tape to cut, insert, add or reorganize at a later date. You can use colored pens to mark important sections.
- Use clear plastic inserts to store documents, clippings, or snapshots.

ORGANIZING A JOURNAL

Like many creative people, Leo Tolstoy kept a journal and used the materials from his journals to write his published works. He divided his journal into two parts. In one he recorded outward events of each day. In the other, he wrote about the inner significance of these events. This pattern of dividing a journal into parts or sections has been expanded by a psychologist, Ira Progoff, who conducts intensive journal workshops all over the United States. Progoff divides the journal into sixteen sections. Journal entries are written on lined, binder paper and placed into a loose-leaf binder with sixteen brightly colored dividers.

You may not want to use this highly structured approach. However, you might try dividers with headings that fit your own interests. For example, the artistic journal-keeper can have a section for sketches, drawings, cartoons, or designer clothes. The musician might have a section for jotting down melodies or lyrics. The numbers of divisions in a journal can be as varied as the interests of each individual.

To organize your journal, you may find the following structure useful. Or you can create your own structure.

- *Daily log:* Record your daily activities, mail received or sent, phone calls made or received, work activities, social activities. Write about what you did, where you went, and other ways you spent your time. Picture yourself as the captain of a ship keeping a log—a record of what happens.
- *Life history:* If you have one, include a family tree or begin a genealogy chart. Add stories you have heard about your ancestors, and include detailed descriptions of family members who have been important influences in your life. Chapter 3 exercises can be included in this section.

- *My body:* Includes entries about your health and physical activities—diet, exercise, athletics, sports,—information to keep your body in the best possible shape. Write about your gestures, voice, posture, and how you walk; also include nonverbal messages others send. Exercises from Chapter 5 belong in this section.

- *My emotions:* Include entries about habitual emotional responses—old feeling patterns that you notice. In Chapter 6 you will find vocabulary to express your feelings. Write about emotional ambivalence and internal conflicts. Search for hidden feelings and discover your emotional style. Exercises from Chapter 6 belong in this section.

- *My language:* Chapter 7 gives you the opportunity to observe how you use and abuse words. Certain words and expressions block change. Language can freeze and limit your perceptions and responses. The language of "right/wrong" creates defensiveness. Notice when you over-generalize or stereotype. Language can limit growth or expand and open windows to self-discovery. Exercises in Chapter 7 belong in this section.

- *My thoughts:* Explore your beliefs, biases, and prejudices. Begin to notice and question areas in which you have closed your mind. Discover areas of self-deception. Look at your expectations. Expecting too little can lead to boredom; expecting too much can lead to disappointment. Notice old thought patterns that lead to intellectual blocks and find new directions through creative problem-solving. Exercises from Chapter 8 belong in this section.

- *My behavior:* Notice roles you play as you act out a variety of different "selves" in different situations with different people. Expand your awareness of how you manipulate yourself and others, and how you cooperate when others manipulate you. Set goals, make decisions, and put those agendas into action. Explore ways to give up nonproductive behavior patterns and replace them with effective alternatives. Exercises from Chapter 9 belong in this section.

- *Relationships:* Write about family, friends, colleagues, and significant others. You may be socially intelligent at work, yet have difficult relationships at home. Write a list of communication problems and explore ways to break through walls between yourself and others. Find different ways to resolve conflicts. Discover what works best for you in your relationships and how to create constantly changing levels of intimacy or commitment. Chapters 10 and 11 will be helpful for this section.

- *Transcendence:* Expand your awareness of transitions in your life—moving from one stage to the next, from one set of values to another. Creative use of meditation, fantasy, dreams, and guided imagery are important activities that contribute to creative imagination. Explore spiritual and philosophical aspects of your life. Use Chapter 12 to map the inner journey you wish to take to greater wisdom.

- *My special section:* This "Special Section" can be labeled "Miscellaneous". In it you can write or collect any special interests or a mixture of many of your interests. One student compiles quotes.

> *It is a good thing for an uneducated man to read books of quotations.*
> Winston Churchill

For centuries books of quotations have been popular because they offer sparkling gems of wit and wisdom. Wisdom encompasses education, knowledge, experience, sound judgment, understanding, morality and truth. Quotes provide superbly phrased thoughts that help us express our own ideas and feelings. Speakers and writers often use humorous quotes as an icebreaker before presenting a message. Humor is often a facet of wisdom.

Many students say quotes stimulate their thinking and help them start writing. You can respond to or debate quotations. You can relate a quotation to your personal experiences or your observations of others. The literary cadence of the shortest quotations may prompt you to contemplate your personal values. You can make independent judgments about quotations. They may amuse, impress, or exasperate you. The inspired words of great thinkers from the past often include contradictions that contribute to our understanding of the timeless and universal qualities in ourselves. Because quotes provide us with material for our journals, this edition of *Communicating with Myself: A Journal* contains a wealth of famous quotes to stimulate thinking and writing.

REREADING YOUR JOURNAL

After you write in your journal, set it aside. In a few days or weeks, go back and read what you have written. If you wrote from your heart, you will be surprised by some things you wrote. You might want to write down these responses. Notice patterns in your analysis. Also ask yourself questions about the effectiveness of your journal writing. Questions serve as goals toward which to strive. Don't expect to reach them all. Choose a few questions and when those are under control, move on to others.

Ask yourself the following questions when rereading your journal entries. The depth of each question will become clearer each time you return to your journal.

- Have I said what I really think and feel or what I've been taught to think and feel?
- Have I told not only *what happened* but *how I feel* about what happened and *what it means* to me?
- Am I hiding behind impersonal facts or borrowed opinions?
- Am I keeping a distance from myself by focusing on the external world in my writing?
- Are my thoughts and feelings like worn-out cliches about other people and things?
- Am I too critical of myself, my writing, other people?

- Have I been overly sentimental about my past and buried my memories under nostalgia?
- At the other extreme, have I minimized my emotions or buried them in the past without resolving them?
- Have I been as candid as I can be?
- Have I fallen into self-deception about my motives or intentions?
- When the truth is unpleasant, do I use defense mechanisms to hide the truth from myself?
- How have I handled ambivalence in my emotions and contradictions in my attitudes toward myself and others, my life and my beliefs?
- How consistent have I been in my thoughts, feelings, and behavior?
- Have I been as concrete as possible and used specific examples to illustrate my abstract statements?
- Have I shared my strengths, weaknesses, and my humanness with myself by accepting and affirming myself with positive statements?

The purpose of questioning what you write in your journal is to find self-understanding.

Today many of us, at times, experience a feeling of displacement or estrangement. We often don't know why we said something or why we did something. Often we can't remember what happened the day before yesterday. Our lives need continuity.

Each of us is searching for a new vision of life so that we can make a contribution to the future and to society as a whole. The journal is a self-recording device. In journal writing you will find the opportunity to live life in the moment and again in retrospection and this will bring out the full flavor of life's meaning.

I do not see things as they are; I see things as I am.
Anonymous

2

Perception And Context

No human being experiences the world directly. A new born's sense receptors are bombarded by both internal and external stimuli. The baby's nervous system receives all this input—the discomforts of hunger and wetness, the external lights and voices—without being able to create any meaning from it all. In fact, a baby does not perceive its self as a separate entity. *Perception is the process of interpreting sensory stimulation according to individual experience* and it is learned over time. The key words are *sensory, experience,* and *interpretation.*

SENSORY RECEPTORS

> *When one door closes, another opens;
> but often we look so long at the closed door
> that we do not see the one which has
> been opened for us.*
>
> Helen Keller

In addition to the five senses *sight, hearing, touch, taste, and smell,* we may have other senses that haven't yet been identified, labeled, defined, or measured. One individual's sense receptors differ from those of every other individual. The amounts, degrees, and qualities of sights, sounds, odors, and other sensations will differ from one person to another. For example, color blindness, nearsightedness and farsightedness illustrate ranges of color and distance reception. Similarly, hearing ranges of tone and volume vary from one person to the next. In spite of this knowledge, we continue to believe that everyone experiences the world as we perceive it.

Also a person's sensory abilities differ since health, age, and other variables affect what our senses can receive at different times in our lives. Yet an individual is seldom aware of these gradual changes over time.

These questions will help expand your awareness of sense receptors:

- Individuals develop preferences in sense receptors. Do you learn best through hearing or seeing? Are you primarily a visual or an auditory learner?

- Describe your own sense of hearing, sight, smell, touch, and taste. People who make their living tasting wine develop a keen sense of taste. Have you developed one sense over others?

- Begin to become more aware of your senses. Write about them. Have you ever been aware of a change in one of your sense receptors? (A head cold not only blocks your sense of smell but may also affect your hearing.) Changes in sight and hearing are so gradual that people who finally get glasses or a hearing aid often are not aware of these transitions in sense reception.

- In addition to blocking out body awareness (foot going to sleep) and attention awareness (driving by an intended freeway exit), list some personal examples of when you screened out sensory stimuli. (Shut out a speaker, a friend. . . .)

We are bombarded with stimuli every second. Since it is physically impossible to respond simultaneously to all of this stimuli, the brain acts as a "reducing valve". It screens out most incoming stimuli and admits only those of importance at that moment (which may not be as important at another time). The mind often shuts out both internal and external sensations. Our greatest poverty is the poverty of unawareness.

Recording your perceptions will enhance your abilities to perceive more by expanding your awareness of your environment.

- Look at and describe your favorite chair. Notice that you discover more about that chair as you describe it.

- Look at and describe your favorite picture. Notice that you discover more about that picture as you describe it.

Make a daily habit of describing things you see, hear, and touch. The more that you detail a description of something while you are perceiving it, the more of it you will perceive.

EXPERIENCE

Half of the delight of experiencing is to know what you are experiencing.

Jessamyn West

An experience is an instance of encounter with something—actually living and participating in an event through sensation, feeling, or expression. If a personal experience is followed by reflection and examination, skill or practical wisdom follows. Although the senses respond to stimuli, these stimuli have little meaning until we interpret and structure them into a personal framework. Each of us creates a different representation of what is out in the world based on our personal experiences.

In addition to the selectivity made by our nervous systems, our social experiences also restrict what we perceive. Language, which differs with each culture, limits what we can see. Although the eye can distinguish thousands of different shades of color, one culture with a greater number of words for different shades perceives more colors. Eskimos who can distinguish many different kinds of snow and Arabs who can name dozens of different kinds of horses can perceive added variations. A person interested in cars may be able to name dozens of different brands, models, and types while another person who is not interested in cars probably doesn't perceive differences in door handles, hub caps, hood ornaments and such.

Although words are important, vocabulary may be one of the least important differences in the prisons of language. Concepts of time and space differ from one culture to another; some cultures do not have language for past or future. Thus we cannot think like people of other cultures because our perceptions differ. Also each of us has had a different family environment. Although three children may be born to one set of parents, the children differ in birth order. Oldest children differ from middle and last born children. An only child differs from children with siblings. In addition to different family experiences, every child has had different educational experiences regardless of whether they attended the same school or had the same teacher. Ambitious students think more in future time while less interested students concentrate on the present. Differences in cultural, social, and personal experiences are greater than we can count or measure.

Once our nervous systems selectively filter sensory stimuli and our social experiences filter still further, each of us selects from what is out there and filters it a third time through personality screens. Each of us has different perceived needs, values, and expectations. Thus no two human beings perceive reality in the same way. In fact, no single individual perceives the same scene exactly the same way twice. The first time a person stands before the Parthenon or the Taj Mahal is an experience he or she can never duplicate.

INTERPRETATION

Each age of life is new to us;
no matter how old we are,
we still are troubled by inexperience.
    La Rochefoucauld

Each of us creates our individual worlds from the information we receive through our senses and from our unique life experiences. Until we understand and admit that we do not operate directly on the world, but instead on our individual interpretations of it, we will not understand our communication breakdowns. We filter out most of what exists because we can't take it all in. In addition what we do allow in through our personal filters will be interpreted differently by each of us at different times.

One serious problem that separates us from each other is that even though we "know" that each of us differs in sensory reception, we still expect others to see what we see, hear what we hear, experience what we experience, believe what we believe, and value what we value. And we feel threatened by someone who sees, believes, and values what we do not. We can learn to accept the fact that we have no control over how others perceive what we say or do. *Perceptions are inside people not outside in things and events.*

EXPLORING PERCEPTION

> *Vision is the art of seeing things invisible.*
> *Swift*

Familiarity causes us to see things according to our personal biases. The result is that we do not see things as they are. When we search for words to capture and communicate our experiences, we discover that language is the medium through which we clarify and express our uniqueness.

You can observe the language process by which you perceive and experience your world through writing.

- Describe a time when you realized your memory distorted the past (perhaps deleted or overemphasized certain information).

- Describe a time when you and someone you know were at the same event but described what happened or what was said so that an outsider might think you were talking about different events. (A movie? A book? Some other event?)

- Can you describe an experience without distorting it in some way?
- What kinds of a home life did you have as a child? What values were predominant? What political or religious views were held by your parents?

These past experiences have influenced your self-image, your self-esteem, and your values.

Conflicting Perceptions

> *If one would improve the perception of others,
> then let him look to his own performance.*
> Leonard Read

Humans tend to see things as complete. We fill in missing lines and dots, words and ideas. We see things as constant, the same as they were before. We also see things in context—what surrounds things. For example a gray square on black looks light while the same gray square on white looks dark. We have preconceptions—mental sets—and we see things in set patterns.

In spite of these human perceptual tendencies, individual differences influence our reception of noise, size, movement, intensity, contrast and novelty. One generation can't stand the music of the next or last generation. Also perceptions differ from one social class to another. A silver dollar looks larger to a poor child than to a rich one.

When we realize that perception is selective, that we fit new perceptions into old patterns, and that external variables affect perception, we begin to understand how others perceive different realities from our own—even in the same situation. Among the many influences that create different perceptions, individual modes of *selectivity* are based on:

1. physiological differences (seeing, hearing, and so on)
2. psychological differences (interests, values, personality)
3. experiential differences (birth order, education, culture)
4. contextual differences (time, age, relationship)

Although we can never end *all* communication breakdowns, we can become more conscious of these individual differences in perception.

How I perceive you is not who you are. How you perceive me is not who I am. The following suggestions can help you become more aware of conflicting perceptions.

- At the end of one Sunday, ask each person in your household to tell you their version of how each member of the family spent their day.

   Write down the names of each person (mother, father, wife, child . . .). Mother writes a brief description of what she, father, and each person did and said. Father writes descriptions of what each family member did and said. Others do the same.

   Compare these different perceptions of what was said and done in one family on just one day.

- Go to a movie with three or more friends. *Before* discussing the movie, ask each person to write their impressions.

- Start family discussions of memories—past impressions of events or people. Start a list of perceptual differences.

    (Sister #1 says, "Dad was the knight on the white horse!" Sister #2 says, "He was a wimp!")

- Write about a conflict you have had between your view of yourself and another person's view of you.

- Describe your feelings about this discrepancy.

- How did you handle this discrepancy? Did you have other choices?

- Write about a conflict you are having with another person in which you each view your relationship differently.

- Begin a record of perception conflicts.

    (John feels school is a waste of time. Bill perceives it as valuable. Mike finds Mary fascinating. Rick finds her boring.)

    "You are wrong" simply means, "I'm not seeing what you are seeing."

Once we internalize these differences in perception, we won't get defensive when another person differs with us or contradicts us. We will expect each person to see and experience everything differently.

Changing Perceptions

> *This is my way . . . What is your way?*
> *THE WAY doesn't exist.*
>   *Friedrich Nietzsche*

Perceptions change over time. When you are eight, going camping in the mountains for the first time will never be the same again. How we perceive our parents when we are five differs from how we see them at twelve or fourteen. A young child sees a parent as an omnipotent, all-seeing, all-knowing, godlike being. In the teens, our parent images change drastically, often harshly, but they are still subject to individual interpretation. How we perceive a friend when we first meet changes as we get to know each other.

Perceptions are not static but constantly changing.

- Describe a perception you had of a person years ago. How has your perception of that person changed? Example: A twelve year old describes his mother:

   My mother doesn't like to get up in the morning. She says she has insomnia, so she reads late into the night—romance novels and True Confessions. *I have been getting up by myself since I started kindergarten. I feed and dress myself. I'm glad my mother doesn't get up; she's crabby in the morning. I think she doesn't like children. She has colds, hay fever, and headaches all the time. She hates housework and gets out of the house when she gets up at about noon. She goes to movies or plays volleyball, or goes anywhere to get out of the house.*

   (Ten years later, the same individual, describes the same mother after her death.)

   My mother was her best self in the evenings. She taught us to play Monopoly, poker and other card games. On weekends, we played tennis and went for hikes through Golden Gate Park in San Francisco. Even though we lived on a limited income, she planned short vacations. When my cousins were out of work, my mother took them in. One time, she felt sorry for her younger sister and bought her a new dress even though we didn't have much money.

- What kinds of perceptions have you created of your parents? Of other significant persons in your life? Do you tend to create negative or positive images?

- Write some impressions of different people you meet for the first time. In six months or a year, check for changes from your first perceptions.

- Write about an experience or an interpretation of something that has changed.

- Write about some perception that presently seems to be in the process of changing. (School? A job? A relationship?)

When we become more aware that each of us is constantly in transition, we will understand that another person's perceptions of us are continuously, often unconsciously, changing.

When we internalize the fact that we create our perceptions, that perceptions are not in objects, situations, or people, we will know that what people say tells more about *them* than it tells about what they are describing.

Choose among these goals; I want to . . .

- work toward less biased perceptions
- become more conscious of distortions, deletions, selections
- learn more about how perception works
- explore the idea that there may not be such a thing as "Reality" or "The Truth"
- explore the idea that for many questions there are many answers and for some questions there may not be any answers

Every historian writes history through his/her selective perceptions. Every scientific discovery comes through a scientist's personal perceptions. Perception is personal, social, cultural, and global. In every chapter in this book, we will again remind ourselves how perception affects our feelings, thoughts, and behavior; how it affects our relationships, our work, and every aspect of our lives.

EXPLORING CONTEXT

Most of us are familiar with the concept of verbal context. For example, if a friend tells you a reviewer commenting on a book said, "superb style", you might want to read the book. However, the reviewer wrote: "The author's superb style can not cover up a weak plot and poor character development." Taking words *out of context* means taking out a part of something from a larger structure. Taking something out of context often leads to distortion.

A context consists of a group of details that form some sort of structure that makes sense as a whole. The whole is always more than the sum of its parts. During every waking minute, all the nerve endings in our eyes, ears, nose, and skin receive more sights, sounds, odors, and tactile sensations than we can process so our brain screens out most signals. Each of us lets different signals in depending upon the context—we add our life experiences to the situation. When introduced to a new person, you might notice eyes and hair while another person listens to a voice and remembers a name.

Context can produce opposite reactions in a single person. If you can put your right hand in ice water and your left hand in hot water, then put both hands into lukewarm water, the right hand will experince the lukewarm water as hot while the left hand will experience the lukewarm water as cold. We are often puzzled by our own inconsistent reactions but this simple experiment illustrates how context can affect our reactions to an experience that might be enjoyable at one time and irritating at another.

Context also affects social situations. We often interpret the present based on past experiences. If you see a friend frown, you might think, "She doesn't like what I am saying." Your father always frowned when he disagreed with you. If you say to your frowning friend, "Do you disagree with what I am saying?" The friend might say, "Sorry I have a headache." In order to know more about how people perceive, think, and communicate within a particular context, we need more information. Some of this information comes through asking questions.

Culture as Context

On a more complex level, culture is a context that includes race, religion, and all the variables of time and place. In the Old West, the Indian who stole the most horses became the tribal chief; yet among the white pioneers, a horse thief was hanged. Anthropologists study human beings in different social groups and write about their different rules, laws, customs, and institutions. The life history of an individual is an accommodation to the patterns and standards handed down in his or her specific social community.

From the moment of birth, the customs into which we are born shape our feelings and thoughts, our language and behavior, our habits and beliefs, our values and experiences. For example, our language is made up of opposites: high low, near far, fast slow, large small, rich poor, hot cold. Yet each of these words is relative to its context. We feel hot when the room temperature reaches 80 degrees. The oven is hot when it reaches 350 degrees. Most opposites sit on the ends of a continuum and are relative to the situation that includes the cultural context.

Each society teaches its members what to feel and how to think. Ake Daun, professor at Stockholm University, is writing a book called *The Swedish Mentality.* He uses psychological and sociological studies that measure and compare the emotional responses of different nations. Daun says that Swedes give a low value to emotion and a high value to rationality. In Sweden strong emotions are suppressed or repressed. He notes for example that there is no Swedish equivalent of the French phrase "crime of passion."

In 1963, fifty-three percent of adult Americans admitted to crying after the murder of President John F. Kennedy. When Prime Minister Olaf Palme was assassinated in 1986, only twenty-four percent of adult Swedes admitted crying. The Swedes take pride in placing a rational mind above sentimental feelings. Many outsiders see Swedes as difficult to reach, difficult to make friends with, and somewhat cold and impersonal. Every culture differs from every other.

The cultural context is the framework within which we form judgments, attitudes, beliefs, and values. These cultural differences affect our relationships with others. Marriages between two people from different cultures often result in conflict. Similar misunderstandings occur in relationships between those of different races, religions, sexes, and age groups. Even in a single family, birth order and personality differences may result in conflict. The more we become aware of and recognize political, social, and personal contextual differences, the fewer will be the communication barriers between and among us. The more we accept these differences, the more successfully we can accommodate them. Anthropologist Edward T. Hall contends that *culture is communication.* We interpret or send a message from our cultural knowledge—which includes all those things we know and take for granted. Since this pervasive knowledge informs and shapes our messages and responses, it is our communication. *Communication can not be separated from its cultural context.*

The word culture refers to an entire system of socially created and transmitted beliefs, ideas, and patterns of behavior. The system includes thoughts, language, actions, and knowledge (science, history, literature, art, religion, philosophy) specific to a particular society. We learn posture, appearance, dress, as well as individual expressions of emotions, thoughts and actions. Becoming aware of how our cultural context affects us is a lifelong process that we will never quite complete.

A child born into a culture enters life center stage in the middle of a play. The play has a script that the child must learn—the names of objects, the meaning of events, the values, and ethical standards, the laws and social systems that already exist. The goal is to live life in the fullest, amplest sense, within the context of the culture into which he or she is born.

Context provides the foundation upon which we create our individual perceptions of reality, our personal values and goals. *Context includes the total situation, background, environment and all that is relevant to a particular event, personality, or creation.* Wisdom in human understanding of self and others requires consciousness and understanding of perception and context.

Awareness of Context

We often live our lives without realizing what is happening. Unaware of the complexities inherent in being human, we give our lives little more attention than we give to breathing. *Awareness is a skill.* It can be developed. To be aware is to wake up to possibilities, to be more attuned to our own thoughts and feelings, to be more in touch with our bodies, to be more responsible for our behavior.

When things happen within us or around us without our awareness, we limit our lives. Ultimately, we are responsible for the choices we make, including the choice to be more conscious. Responsibility begins with a willingness to acknowledge that we are the source of what we are, what we do, and what we have. Although we can never know enough, we are still responsible. We can choose to take ownership of our own lives.

In our culture, we have learned methods to escape freedom and responsibility. We use expressions like, "I didn't know." "I forgot." "It wasn't my fault." "He told me to do it." If I get a ticket for driving 25 mph in a 15 mph zone, the judge will not accept my statement that I did not know I was driving through a school zone. Ignorance of the law is no excuse.

Free choice is both a gift and a curse. Given the freedom to choose, we find that excuses don't work. Moralistic language—good/bad, right/wrong, should/shouldn't—creates guilt, anger, and resentment in ourselves and others as the body stiffens in defense. Also, medical language—sick/well, neurotic/normal, ill/healthy—creates anxiety and depression. Saying, "Well, I had a headache," or "I didn't feel well" may be statements of fact but do not change what happened or the choices we made. We lose some critical comprehension of what is happening in the context of certain situations if we try to escape the consequences of our choices.

Awareness of language patterns passed from one generation to another as a vehicle to avoid responsibility can help us break the cycle. Once aware of such programming, we need not teach it to our children. Set against this background of perception and context, we now proceed to explore the individual *self.*

Journal writing offers you an opportunity to select a goal for the purpose of making some aspect of your life work better. Choose one goal from this list. Then, on a separate sheet of paper write in more detail how you plan to make your life different.

- To understand myself (my values, interests . . .) better
- To improve my self-esteem; to feel more confident
- To resolve problems in my relationships—family/friends/work
- To improve my ability to relate to people in general
- To acquire coping skills through relaxation and imagery
- To learn self-assertion, time or financial management

- To develop better control over emotions (be more specific)
    1. feel less anxious and/or depressed
    2. control anger and resentment
    3. feel less guilt and/or inadequacy
- To improve my behavior—self-control of eating, drinking, or drug-taking
- To improve handling of stress or pressures in general
- To improve thinking, judgment, and objectivity
- To improve my body through nutrition and exercise
- To find more significance or meaning in my life
- To have realistic expectations of myself and others

I do not expect anyone else to make my life better. My expectations of myself, given a reasonable time, are realistic. I expect of myself a high level of commitment to expanding self-awareness and a concerted effort to move closer to my goals. I expect to become more aware of defensiveness and self-deception. I do not expect to find answers to all of my personal or relationship problems or to find answers to many of life's mysteries. I want to ask questions and explore different possibilities, to become more aware of how my perceptions and the contexts of my life affect the ways in which I create my personal reality.

*Only when I know who I am
will I know what is possible.*
Baba Ram Dass

3
Creating Self-Concept

The simple edict "know thyself" is so complex and difficult that complete self-knowledge remains a goal rather than a reality. The study of self is continuous as long as one lives. Even small steps toward self-knowledge can lead to a more satisfying life. Although we may not have all the information about ourselves necessary to make the best decisions, and even though our lives are continuously in flux, each of us is responsible for the choices we make and the lives we lead.

Self-knowledge leads to autonomy and personal power which contributes to a rich inner life and free human spirit. A scientist works to take something apart; an artist to put something together. In the process of studying the self, we will first look at the parts then synthesize them into a whole. Self-knowledge, the foundation of wisdom, can eventually lead us to self-esteem through social contributions to the world.

YOUR HISTORICAL PAST

The search for self requires a coherent picture: knowledge of the past, observation of the present, and vision of the future. Every human is born into a family. Collecting and organizing family information gives family members a deeper sense of self through an understanding of their roots. Humans have a "passing on" impulse which takes various forms. Some families keep records in a family Bible. Often an older family member has worked on a family tree with names and dates of births, marriages, and deaths of past family members. Some people trace their family lines through the study of *genealogy*. Genealogy charts provide us with the facts of our historical past.

Other forms of passing on family history include collections of letters, journals, diaries, and photographs. If you are fortunate, you may find collections of these. Make copies. In a box, gather together birth certificates, school diplomas, marriage licenses, military records, letters, and written materials. Using an audio or videotape, interview older relatives. If you don't do it *now*, a death could mean you may never get another chance. Ask older relatives some questions from different chapters in this journal. After collecting tapes of interviews and family records, begin to write your personal records.

Family Memories

Memory is the mother of all wisdom.
Aeschylus

Some items listed here may not fit your family; others may be unimportant. Delete those and add your own special memories. Include important people not listed here.

In some degree of detail, write about:

- Relatives born before your grandparents

- Family legends that have been passed down

- Memories you have of your grandparents

- The stories they told you

- Your feelings when you were with them (Did you feel proud of or embarrassed by them? Did you feel close or distant?)

- The good times and the bad times

- The fun and the disappointments

- Your expectations of your grandparents (Did you expect too much or too little? What did your grandparents give you?)

- Your father's family (From where did they originate?)

- What did they do? Where does the family name come from? Name the children and birth order. What stories did your father tell about his childhood? Do you have a favorite aunt? uncle? What do you remember about cousins?)

- Your mother's family (From where did they originate?)

- Some family reunions, holidays, special occasions

- Divorces, illness, deaths, family tragedies

Talk to other family members. You will discover that what we remember is not necessarily the way it was and that is O.K.

PHOTO-ANALYSIS

A study of old photographs provides an opportunity to discover new information about the self and the family. Photos are mirrors with memories.

To discover hidden stories in photographs:

- Go to the family album. Choose several family photos that represent different groups of people. For example, pictures of your grandparents with their children, pictures of your parents when they were children, pictures of your parents with you and your siblings, pictures of you as a baby and pictures of you at different ages.

- Describe your social and cultural background.

Chapter 3: Creating Self-Concept   **33**

- Describe the setting and the background of the picture. What was the occasion?

- What is your immediate impression? Who and what do you see?

- What feelings does this picture invoke in you?

- Note physical intimacy. Is there touching? How?

- How do people in the photo feel about their bodies? (Embarrassed, proud, showing off, hiding, seductive, etc.)

- What emotions are expressed? (Shy, aloof, suspicious, bright, bored, distant, friendly, depressed, anxious, lonely.)

- If there is a group, is there harmony or chaos? Who has the power or the attention? Do you see affection there?

- Learn to read the photo like a book. Look at each individual face. What is obvious? What is subtle?

- In a series of photos, do you see any patterns? (Emotional states, personality expressions, intimacy patterns.) For example, who usually stands next to whom? Who holds the baby? What are the distances between the subjects.

- Have you changed? How? Have you remained the same? How?

- Let your mind go back to the time when the photo was taken. What do you recall of that time in your family history?

- Using the approximate date or year when the picture was taken, allow your mind to dwell on any personal, social or historical events of that time.

Ask older relatives to show you their photo collections. They will tell you stories about your family. Write down names and dates.

Childhood Memories

Personal myth is based on family myths—all the stories we tell others about ourselves. These personal myths are often unconsciously colored by our absorption of cultural and family memories as well as by the responses of others when we reveal our thoughts and feelings. We tend to forget some things and remember others.

Generally we forget names of things, people, numbers, and dates. We often forget unpleasant things, facts that don't fit our beliefs. We tend to forget our failures or things we don't understand. We tend to remember what we believe to be worth remembering, what interests us, what things we do or use frequently, or what we are motivated to remember.

Make time to record your personal memories of yourself and your family. Journals, letters, and autobiographies are collected in public libraries, and state and national archives.

- What is your earliest memory? How old were you at that time?

- When you were a child, how did you feel about your mother? Have those feelings changed? How? Write details.

- When you were a child, how did you feel about your father? Have those feelings changed? How? Write details.

- Write about your brothers and sisters—names, birth order, birth dates. Are you oldest, youngest, middle or only child? What was it like to be the oldest (youngest, middle, or only child)? If you had brothers or sisters, write childhood memories of them. Include your feelings.

EXCERPT FROM A JOURNAL

As the first daughter, I was born two years and ten months before my baby sister. She was a sickly baby and my mother worried about her. Mother constantly told me to be quiet and sent me to my grandmother. As time went on, when we went some place as a family, my mother always took the baby; my dad always took my hand. I came to the conclusion that my mother loved the baby best.

Although I felt replaced, I loved my little baby sister very much. Even though she grew to be a chubby little two year old, I worried for fear she might die. During our growing-up years, I had mixed feelings about my baby sister. I felt I had been pushed out by her at the same time that I felt very protective of her. This ambivalence, which I did not understand, caused me a great deal of discomfort.

My mothering feelings toward my baby sister contributed to my wanting babies. I had six healthy nine pounders but always worried that they might die. Being the oldest daughter created in me a protective, mothering personality, the desire to have children, and a competitive drive to be first in school and work. Position in the family has had dramatic effects on my personality.

Do You Know Your Parents?

It's possible to spend hours a day with someone for years and not know that person—father, mother, child, spouse.

Fold a piece of paper down the middle. Write a heading on the left half "My Father." Write a heading on the right half "My Mother." Under these columns write answers to these questions:

- Where was he/she born? Birth date? Position in the family?
- Where and when did he/she go to school? To what grade?
- As a child, what did he/she want to be as an adult?
- What was his/her first full-time job?
- How did your parents first meet?
- What did they do on their first date?
- Where, when, how did they get married?
- Among his/her friends, who are the closest/best friends?
- What is his/her favorite food? What foods don't they like?
- What part of the newspaper do they read first?
- What is his/her favorite TV show? Movie?
- What is his/her political party?
- What does your father/mother value?
- What does your father/mother want out of life?
- If parents are divorced—when, where, under what circumstances?

When you reread what you have written you may have unanswered questions that older family members can answer.

Adult children often complain that their parents don't know who they are, what they want, and what is important to them. If you want your parents to know you, you can exchange some of the above information about yourself with them. Make a family game of these questions and share with each other what you don't already know. Do it now! One day it will be too late!

Many of us tend to be overly critical of our parents. Resolving negative feelings about our parents contributes to our personal growth and maturity. The goal is to unify and construct images of our parents as whole human beings—neither good nor bad, but human.

YOUR MOTHER IMAGE

You have selectively put together an image of your mother based on past perceptions and experiences. She is not now the mother you had when you were ten or will have when you are older. What was your mother like when you were ten? What is your mother like as you perceive her today?

- Begin with weaknesses, bad habits, prejudices, faults—include negative feelings she expresses about herself, you, and others in the family. How does she deal with conflict? Emotions? Failures? Problems?

- Now write about her strengths, positive qualities, good habits, good feelings she has about herself, you, others; satisfactions, pleasures, happiness she expresses. What has your mother given you that you value?

- Write about the emotional reactions you experienced as you wrote these images of your mother. One purpose of this activity is to unify these two images—positive and negative—into a whole person, neither good nor bad, but simply human.

YOUR FATHER IMAGE

Go through the same process with your father—your father image. Become more aware that your perceptions and feelings are images that you have created. No one else in the world perceives your parents as you do.

Make a list called "Gifts My Mother (Father) Gave Me." Gifts can come from learning what you don't want in life. For example, some young people born into families of incredible wealth walk away and leave behind them everything that money can buy to find their own values and purposes for living. The oldest daughter of the Marx Toys family, (whose father's purpose in life was to make money) founded an organization to better social conditions. The son of the wealthy owner of the Baskin-Robbins ice-cream chain became a vegetarian and wrote, A Diet To Save the World. And the oldest son of a famous tobacco family found his purpose in life fighting for "A Smoke Free World."

You can love your parents and still be free to find your own life paths. Integrating your parent-images can help you relate to your "past" parent with acceptance. Your parent-images are not of "real" persons but ones you create by selectively putting together images out of your own needs and expectations as both a child and an adult. Accepting your parents requires maturity and compassion. It means giving up making excuses for personal problems.

Self-acceptance follows acceptance of parents. You no longer need to live up to some fantasy image you believe your parents had of you. Their approval of you would be nice to have, but you can be happy with or without it. If you choose to hang on to your grievances against your parents, ask yourself, "What do I gain by clinging to my anger at my mother/father?" "What do I gain by being unforgiving?"

Disappointment in parental love comes from grieving for a mythical loss of an ideal family love that has never existed. In many cultures, children were historically murdered, abused, unwanted, and mistreated. For farmers, children were an extra pair of hands. The American frontier was a sad, lonely place for both children and parents of the West and they lived a cruel life. Children are often unlovable, untrainable creatures. To be forgiving of human frailties—our own and others—we can begin by forgiving our parents for being human, for being imperfect. Only when we acknowledge human tragedy as a striving for human perfection can we hope to find our better selves.

Childhood perceptions and memories contribute to your self-image.

- What did you do in order to be accepted or loved by your parents?

- List the things you were told to do or be. For example: Be polite! Be quiet! Be honest! Be clean and neat! (Listen to the voice in your head. Whose voice is it?)

Chapter 3: Creating Self-Concept   39

- List the things you were told *not* to do or be. For example: Don't be stupid! Don't be lazy! Don't touch! Don't cry!

- List the needs your mother had for your behavior. For example: Eat everything! Be quiet! Be neat/clean!

- List the needs your father had for your behavior. For example: Be a man (lady)! Be brave! Be strong!

- List the needs your brothers or sisters had; your grandparents; any other significant person in your life.

- What did you do in your family to make people pay attention to you? How did you get people to do what you wanted?

- What was the number one rule in your house?

- Would you describe your family as close-knit?

If you look deeply, you will discover how you have created your self-image. Retain the positive and accept the negative aspects of that image.

Memories of childhood, whether they are painful or happy, are often imperfect. We create our parent images and self-images from faulty childhood perceptions. From these, we choose what fits the images we wish to create of our parents and ourselves.

THE PRESENT

> *There is no description so difficult as describing oneself.*
> Montaigne

Your self-image comes from the past and moves into the future as a continuous, connected, usually unconscious self-definition. Although we are exploring the foundations for your self-image, the search for self-identity continues for life.

The purpose of this activity is to help you understand that identity is complex—always changing, and shaped both publicly and privately.

- On a sheet of paper, write the date and title, "Who Am I?" Write freely and honestly as long as you can write. Put the paper away for a few days.
- At a later date, take out another sheet of paper. Title it "Who Am I?" Add as much as you can to what you have already written.
- Periodically add and/or change what you have written.

Do you see yourself as you are or as the person you were?

Self-Image

If one of your goals is to know yourself, then you will need time and thought to become a more conscious individual. Thinking and writing will help clarify who you are. Sometimes insights will occur when you are not actively searching for them.

Answers to the following items can be brief. However, you will gain the most by including examples, descriptions, illustrations—by peeling away the levels until you get at the core. Write on separate paper so that you can rewrite answers at a later date.

- Write five words that describe you.

- Describe your personality by writing about yourself.

- List your strengths/talents, your most valuable assets.

- List your weaknesses. What is your worst trait?

- In what ways are you your own worst enemy?

- Do you tend to be too meek or too aggressive?

- What are the two sides of your personality?

- What is the biggest conflict in your personality?

Part 1: Creating Meaning

- List three goals you have for personal improvement.

- Select a color, an animal, a flower that describes you.

- List five nonmaterial things you value most.

- List five material things you value most.

- What do you worry about most? What are you afraid of?

- Who are the most important people in your life today?

- Are you too trusting or too untrusting?

- With whom have you had the biggest conflicts? What were they? How did you handle them?

- Describe one significant relationship.

- Are your standards too high? Too low?

- What parts of your life would you change?

- What was your greatest challenge? Greatest disappointment?

- What was your greatest satisfaction?

- Write about a turning point, a special problem, a lucky break, a bad break, a crisis.

Part 1: Creating Meaning

- Write about a major event that was pleasant.

- Write about a major event that was sad.

- Write about your most embarrassing moment.

- Write about a personal secret.

- What frustrates you the most?

- What is your most serious problem?

- What causes you the greatest daily annoyance?

- What dreams have you fulfilled? What dreams have you not fulfilled.

- What dreams do you have now?

- What are you most proud of? What gives you the greatest joy?

- Write about a peak experience in your life.

- Write about your most intense love experience.

- What are your future plans? What is left unfinished?

- What do you want to do with the rest of your life?

After a few weeks, reread what you have written and write responses to (thoughts and feelings about) those journal entries.

Perhaps you have thoughts and feelings that you want to avoid—thoughts that flee from consciousness whenever you get close. See if you can catch some of them. Title a paper "Personal Information". Put down thoughts and feelings that you have never told anyone. Fantasies, guided imagery, dreams, music and art are other channels that can lead you to your unconscious. Drawings, images, symbols, diagrams, and collages can symbolically represent thoughts, feelings, and experiences.

A COLLAGE

You can get in touch with aspects of yourself through a collage.

- Get a large piece of cardboard or butcher paper. Cut any number of pictures, ads, and words from magazines. Choose pictures of people, animals, objects,—anything that interests you or says something about a quality in you. Choose some nature pictures, some city skyscrapers, whatever attracts you. Include photographs, buttons, beads, feathers—anything that means something to you. Then mount these items on your paper in some pattern or form that appeals to you.

When you are finished, study what you have put together. You will discover some new information about yourself.

Psychologist Abraham Maslow says we are torn between "a need to know" and "the fear of knowing" about ourselves. If your intention is to discover yourself, you will learn (among other things) to be more comfortable in situations which at times feel disorderly, vague, uncertain, or even inaccurate. You will enjoy the search even when you can't find answers. When you feel threatened by the complexities of life, you can always—for the moment—pull inside like a turtle in the shell. But if you stay there, you will not find the safety you seek. When you reach out to others, you find your self reflected back to you.

Self-image begins with the labels given to us as children by others. As an adult, you have the power to accept or reject labels. Ultimately you will tend to label yourself. Be careful of your language. "I am . . ." is a dangerous phrase. It can make you an object like a table or a chair. Change the "I am . . ." to "At this time in my life, I prefer . . ." or "I tend to act as if . . ." You have created and are responsible for your own self-image.

Become aware of your self-made labels.

- What were some personal labels from your past: Angel? Dummy?

- Are you still using those labels? ("Bad little girl.")

- What do you say to yourself when you make a mistake?

- What do you say to yourself when you do something well?

- Do you have some labels you want to stop using?

- What are some labels you want to start using?

Awareness of labels does not *necessarily mean that you stop using them but that you instead consciously choose accurate, positive ones. ("I'm an overachiever! I can do anything I set my mind on doing.")*

    One of the ways we stop our own growth is to use self-fulfilling prophecies. We lock ourselves into certain behaviors with expressions like, "I'm no good at math (spelling)." Negative statements lock us in. We can learn to hear ourselves and change the program to something positive. For example, "Although I did poorly in math when I was in school, I've learned to control my financial life." Or "When I was a kid, I had trouble with spelling, but today I'm a better speller than I used to be and getting better each day."

PERSONALITY TRAITS

Labels are culturally learned and defined. To become more aware of how you have chosen to define yourself, use the following words in any creative way you want—sentences, lists, or groups. For example: 1) "My Most Desirable Traits" 2) "My Least Desirable Traits" 3) "Traits I Have Not Developed but Would Like to Have."

affluent, aggressive, aloof, ambitious, arrogant, authoritarian, loving, stupid, happy-go-lucky, imitative, impulsive, cheerful, romantic, deceitful, forgiving, cruel, scientifically-minded, friendly, quick-tempered, honest, musical, naive, dirty, sincere, unfriendly, forgiving, cold, helpful, sly, hospitable, apathetic, liberal, broad-minded, hostile, loyal, humble, warm, capable, prejudiced, intelligent, uncooperative, responsible, unreliable, clean, passionate, revengeful, practical, alert, snobbish, treacherous, humorless . . . (add your own words)

- What qualities do you look for in others?

- Define those qualities most important to you.

- Give examples of behavior illustrating the traits you desire.

- What undesirable qualities would you not be willing to accept in yourself and/or in others? Define and describe these.

When we define ourselves, we lock ourselves into self-fulfilling prophecies. If the personality label is a negative one, erase or rewrite that label from your mind tapes so you are free to change. Positive labels can be useful in creating self-esteem.

Self-Esteem

> *For self is a sea boundless and measureless.*
> *Kahlil Gabran*

Although at times all of us have negative thoughts and feelings about ourselves or our behavior, we can learn to phrase negative thoughts in positive ways: "I will be more energetic today!" We can choose to focus on our best assets.

Create a sense of personal worth:

- Make a list of times you felt useful.

- Make a list of times you did something well.

- Make a list of times you made someone else feel good.

- Remember a time you did something for *yourself*.

You can dwell on things that make you feel bad or you can create habits that lead to positive thinking and feeling.

> *Defeat may serve as well as victory*
> *to shake the soul and let the glory out.*
> *Edwin Markham*

After you have learned something from a mistake, it is seldom useful to dwell on it. Many of us replay, over and over, conflicts with others, "Why did I (he/she) do (say) that stupid thing?" Imagine your mind is like a light switch. When you find yourself stuck in a negative groove of your mind-record, flip the switch to the off position. It is more productive to make a habit of dwelling on positive feelings, thoughts, and actions. Take one small step at a time. One change influences all the other parts.

Begin by placing yourself on a scale: one (low) to ten (high). Then elaborate using specific, concrete examples.

- How do I feel about myself?

- How do I communicate to others?

- How much do I risk change?

- How much power/control do I have over myself?

Feeling that you have control over your life makes you feel strong. When you feel powerful, you increase your self-esteem.

Change is not created by contented people nor by helpless ones. Power gives us the energy to choose and to be responsible. We can choose to be more aware of how we use language, thoughts, and emotions in productive ways. We can choose through our attitudes, beliefs, and actions to feel good about ourselves.

One paradox researchers have found is that gifted children often have self-esteem problems. The gifted, a minority group, are sometimes mocked by classmates. Feeling like outsiders, the gifted want to belong in a culture that values being average. Also, gifted children tend to be perfectionists—they use tougher standards on themselves than others. While disadvantaged children are seen as needing help to give them equality, the gifted are seen as advantaged and not in need. They often feel out of place, inadequate to meet the expectations of others. Gifted children tend to be intuitive and thinking, future-oriented and objective. They have difficulty handling criticism and need positive strokes *when they are deserved.*

Out of love, our parents gave us a list of rules so that we could live in and be accepted by society. We were told to be on time, to work hard, to save for a rainy day, to be honest, and loving. For the most part, these rules work. If you cut classes all the time, you fail. If you're often late to work, you'll get fired. However, in the process of growing up, none of us can live up to all the rules. At times, we disappoint ourselves. As a result, we have a running monologue in our heads: "I should never have done that . . . I should have . . . I will never be able to be best in . . . I'm always doing things wrong . . . Why can't I do anything right?"

As adults, these monologues play in our minds like old tapes reminding us of all the times we didn't live up to our own expectations. Not one of us grew up getting everything we wanted. Every child has been disappointed and hurt. Most of us feel that we were abandoned, deprived, or unloved at certain times in our lives. We all carry scars into adulthood. But we have the power to erase these old tapes and write statements on our mind tapes that will lead us to live more productive lives.

Not knowing who we are, what we feel, or what we want, we learn to wear masks that cover our real thoughts and feelings. Although masks help defend us against a perceived dangerous world, we wear these disguises until we believe we are the disguises. We become alienated from ourselves and others as we act out how we think we are "supposed" to be. An awareness of appropriate social roles however, is not the same as losing one's identity behind a pretense mask. It is appropriate and, at times, enjoyable to dress, talk, and act according to the different social contexts of home, school, and work.

Spend some time thinking and writing about these questions:

- How can you find out who you really are and what you want?

- How can you learn to be who you are and feel good about yourself?

- How can you encourage another person to discover his/her authenticity and feel good about him/herself?

- How can we preserve and enhance each other's self-esteem?

The ability to see the positive while accepting the negative is the basis for self-esteem. Affirmations—positive statements one tells the self—are valuable tools that can reshape negative attitudes. When we like ourselves, other people tend to like us. When we like others, they tend to like themselves.

Write an affirmation on a card. Carry it in your purse or wallet or tape it on a mirror where you will read it often. Record a three minute affirmation and listen to the tape until the suggestions become part of your consciousness.

- I am committed to the joy of living.
- I am an accepting person who sends out energy to others.
- I give myself permission to express my feelings in a caring way.
- My presence is a gift I give to others.
- I am willing to let others care for me.
- My will to live will keep my body slim and healthy.
- I surround myself with compassionate people.
- I am the master of my life. My life has a wisdom of its own.
- I have the time to accomplish what I want effortlessly.

Create your own affirmations.

Multiple Selves

> *A man has as many different social selves as there are distinct groups of persons about whose opinion he cares.*
> William James

Each of us has many potential selves. Flexible people fit their behavior to the relationship and the situation rather than hold rigidly to a single identity. We can choose to be warm or cold, dominant or submissive, independent or dependent in any given situation. Although attempting to create a *single* self in a relationship fosters standardized behavior, we tend to reward those who are consistent while we punish their variations. But we can learn to reward, or at least accept, inconsistency in ourselves and others. Emerson said: "Consistency is the hobgoblin of little minds." Each of us can learn the degree of consistency that is most true to our own nature.

Write a statement explaining the ways in which you skate back and forth between different aspects of yourself. For example:

> *I am never wholly one person or another but move back and forth on a continuum between tense/relaxed, controlling/extemporaneous, unsure/smooth, scared/excited, thinking/feeling, expecting/surprised, holding back/letting go, confused/clear, serious/humorous, rigid/flexible, pessimistic/optimistic, objective/subjective, off-balance and centered.*

- Write about your intellectual self.

- Write about your physical self.

- Write about your emotional self.

- Write about your spiritual self.

- Write about your social self.

In the movie, "The Many Faces of Eve" one woman slipped in and out of reality, unconsciously playing out different personalities. Although multiple-personality disorders are rare, most of us are conscious of at least some shifting in our masks of identity, and we feel that we can't count on ourselves when we move from one aspect of our personality to another. After we explore different selves, we can accept these different roles as appropriate in different contexts.

Exploring our sub-personalities is another way of becoming aware of the roles we play in response to roles others play. Sub-personalities, like "voices", affect our behavior and responses.

List as many sub-personalities as you can.

- Give each a name: Bossy, Clinging Vine, Bitch, The Martyr, Savior (Rescuer), Hero, Big Daddy, All-Loving Mother, The Missionary, The Preacher, The Wise Old Man/Woman, The Altruist, Mr./Miss Know It All . . .

- Write a general character sketch describing what each personality looks like (facial expressions/body posture), how it behaves, what it says, the sound of its voice.

- What are the needs of each sub-personality? (To be in control or control subversively, to defend itself, to see itself as an all giving/loving person . . . etc.)

- Under what conditions does it emerge?

- Write down the advantages and disadvantages of each role. What does it gain and what does it lose?

- Write a dialogue between two of your sub-personalities. How do they conflict with or confront each other?

Once you become aware of the dynamics of sub-personalities, you will find you don't need them at all. You can give up subversion and self-defense. The ultimate goal is to integrate or unify sub-personalities and fuse the best parts into one.

We often experience a sense of hypocrisy or unreality as we attempt to define, describe, or label ourselves because we have many facets to fit different situations and relationships. If we consciously choose our roles, the sense of hypocrisy, or "divided-self" tends to disappear.

In this chapter you have looked inward and examined who you are based on your historical background, your childhood experiences, your self-concept and self-esteem. Self-esteem depends upon a realistic self-image that you communicate first with yourself and then with others in relationships. Self-understanding and self-acceptance, the foundations for interactions with others, lead to more positive relationships. Few things in life are more directly related to contentment and quality of life than liking the self and others.

The great arc of life stretches from conception to death. Although we can artificially divide the years into sections, inner growth and greater consciousness of the whole individual life is a continuous transition without separations. Each phase of life melds into the last and moves toward a blend of awareness, experience, intelligence, and wisdom. In the next chapter, we will explore life's transitions and how, by defining our values and setting goals, we can choose our future paths.

Nothing endures but change.
Heraclitus

4

Transformation and Change

The concept of change implies stages, steps, or units of difference. Transformation however, most often occurs as an ongoing process—a slow, imperceptible movement, a natural progression similar to life cycles. Sometimes a precipitating event appears to trigger an abrupt change, but this event simply appears as a force that helps a person break through to the next stage.

1. The caterpillar stage—existing state, old roles, comfortable, familiar, secure, controlled.
2. The cocoon stage—some pressure, some dissatisfaction or agitation, a letting go, taking on new, changing tasks, uncontrollable, unpredictable; a withdrawal or running away, feeling "stuck" or aimless, a sense of loss or impending danger.
3. The butterfly stage—with some degree of pain a break-through, new roles, new work, some aspect of a relationship changes, breaking through some confinement into the unknown and unfamiliar, sense of risk as you move into the beginning of another transformation cycle.

Notice these "Stages of Transformation" as natural progressions in your own life. Choose specific examples of each phase and write about them.

- The caterpillar

- The cocoon

- The butterfly

Notice your choices and/or resistance to choosing.

Certain emotions accompany change—misunderstanding, anger, resistance, denial, disbelief, defensiveness. These emotions can be replaced by an attitude of acceptance and self-support, problem-solving, adaptation, and willingness to risk. It's not so much that we're afraid of change or that we love the old ways, but it's that place in between we fear—like being on a trapeze—there's nothing to hold on to. Barriers to change include unawareness, confusion, opposition to concepts presented by others, unwillingness to think about a problem or try alternatives, or attempting a change that fails and being unwilling to abandon it. Cooperating with your transformations requires that you recognize and accept the need for change, predict and identify resistance, develop a strategy for implementing change, manage the process with feedback from your decisions, and evaluate the results.

> *There is nothing more difficult to plan, more doubtful of success, nor more dangerous to manage, than the creation of a new system. For the initiator has the enmity of all who would profit by preservation of the old and merely lukewarm defenders in those who would gain by the new one.*
>
> *Machiavelli*

Change hurts and feels wonderful at the same time. But we cannot refuse to grow. Just as our bodies change physically, new information and life's experiences force us to move emotionally and spiritually. Just as all technology doesn't necessarily bring

progress, not all transitions can be classified as growth. Through experience, we learn when to let go and move on to the next phase of living.
Close your eyes. Relax. Take a deep breath. *Visualize:*

1. Notice the changes that are going on in your life.
2. How do you want the next moment, the next day to be?
3. How do you want your life to be?
4. Feel it as if it's already changed.
5. Share yourself—the love and joy you can express.

Notice that transformation affects chains of interaction between you and your family, friends, co-workers and the accompanying environments.

Human beings have a powerful drive to maintain a sense of identity, a sense of continuity that serves to allay fears of changing or of being changed by outside forces. This drive for safety and control results in a search for certainty, for security based on life being consistent and unchanging. At the same time each of us tries to maintain our identity through controlling change, we also have a powerful drive to be something more than we are now, to fulfill some potential being that we have the capacity to be, that we are not now but hope to become. Each of us can create a personal balance between powerful but opposing drives by skating back and forth between them. A precondition for finding a balance depends upon our willingness to allow them both to exist, to come into our consciousness, and to acknowledge their existence.

One aspect of personal change is to recognize that it takes place within the context of a changing world set in a particular culture. The confusing world in which we live, subject as it is to vast and rapid changes, leaves us with many choices. We can withdraw like a turtle in a shell or we can learn to be at home in this modern world by responding to its extraordinary challenges and tensions. We can accept today's change and variety and even enjoy it if we participate in it and acknowledge the existence of coexisting, incompatible forces.

You are in charge. You choose the amount of change and the rate of change. You can also choose your attitude toward change. Although change produces stress because it requires us to move into the unknown, some people thrive on **eustress**—good stress. They choose life as an adventure that is ongoing, ever changing. Letting go of who you were makes room for becoming who you can be. You may feel sad to leave your past self, but once you find the courage to move, you find energy to go forward.

Simple changes like dressing differently or changing your hair can make those around you uncomfortable. They fear such changes will change the relationship—and it may. The man who says, "My wife is no longer the woman I married" can be happy that his wife at forty is not the same person she was at twenty. Relationships follow their own transformations. When things seem to be "falling apart" they are often falling together. You can't stop change, not in the world nor in your personal life. You can live life to its fullest and achieve a quality of life above what you now live when you welcome change.

To become aware of your transitions, write about these indicators:

- A desire for change

- A feeling of inadequacy in some area (money, body image, health, emotional well-being)

- A growing resentment about something you are doing

- Doing something as a duty or requirement without pleasure

- Feeling depressed

- A preoccupation with something—weight, sex, etc.

- Obvious mental or physical problems

- Feeling guilty about some behavior

Periodically, return to this writing and continue exploring.

PERSONAL VALUES

> *No legacy is as rich as honesty.*
> *Shakespeare*

A question humans have asked since time began is: "What is the good life?" Here is a Greek list:

> *Health is the best that heaven sends*
> *Next, to be comely to look upon*
> *The third is riches, justly won*
> *The fourth to be young among one's friends*

These universal values seem to be timeless. Some values, however, such as freedom and relationships may be antithetical. Yet over a full lifetime we can live our most important values. *Values are preferred outcomes of all our activities.* Often because we don't know who we are, what we feel, or what we want, we have difficulty choosing our values.

Write about the following blocks to finding your values. Note those that you have resisted and then later found to be better values than those you chose.

- Trying to feel what you are told you should feel "You should feel grateful and happy."

- Trying to feel what is socially acceptable to feel "Don't feel hurt, angry, or any other ugly feeling."

- Trying to want what you are told you should want "You should want an education, a good job, a family."

- Trying to want what another person wants you to want "I want you to love me and put me first."

- Trying to want what is socially acceptable to want "You should want money, success, and love."

Notice that what you want changes over time.

You communicate your values through your actions. One way to measure what you value is to chart how you use time. The use of time for one purpose involves the sacrifice of alternatives.

Values and Time

There are one hundred sixty-eight hours in a week. How do you spend your time?

- Begin by estimating how you believe you spend your time on a separate sheet of paper.
- Keep an actual record for one week (see chart).
- Now take a piece of paper and write how you want to spend your time.

Many people feel anxious about time. Time is a symbol for life and can be very significant in illustrating what we value.

Time Log (168 hours in a week)

Time for	Estimated	Mon.	Tues.	Wed.	Thurs.	Fri.	Sat.	Sun.	The Way I Want It
Sleep									
Work									

School
  Classwork
  Homework									

TV, Movies, Entertainment									

Reading
  Papers
  Magazines
  Books									

Grooming
  Dressing
  Hair
  Bath
  Teeth									

Social
  Clubs
  Groups									

Exercise
  Sports
  Other									

Transportation									

Meals
  Eating
  Cooking
  Shopping
  Dishes									

Cleaning
  House
  Clothes									

The arts
  Music
  Drama
  Other									

Business
  Doctor
  Dentist
  Car
  Accounts									

Telephone
  Social
  Business									

Other									

In a section entitled "Time", write the following:

- What do you say about time? ("The clock is running out . . . Passing time . . . Killing time . . . Time is on our side . . . etc.")

- Describe your attitudes/feelings toward time.

- Write about an experience you have had with time distortion. (Clock time is measured in seconds, minutes, hours, days, months, and years. When we are in a hurry, standing in line seems to take forever.)

- Write about an experience when you transcended time.

In an exciting conversation or other experience, you can lose consciousness of where you are, what day or time it is. Inner time is *not* sequential. In retrospective time, the years fly by. Yet introspective time (the moment at hand) sometimes drags.

Time is related to dependability. Lateness suggests low regard for others or the situation. Compulsive or habitual tardiness may be a need to feel special, a need for a sense of control or power, a punishment, an expression of hostility, or a need for attention. Chronic lateness can also be symptomatic of lack of awareness of human limitations, poor self-esteem, a means of manipulating others, a way to rebel against authority, repressed anger, or a test of others to see how much they will put up with. "If you love me, you will put up with my lateness (drinking or other addictions)."

People who are future-oriented usually succeed in the professional and business worlds. They tend to smile more but laugh less. Present-oriented people give more time to relationships, impulses, and enjoying the present at the expense of the future.

Your behavior can tell you what you value.

Values and Money

Money can represent power, security, freedom or any number of other things people want. Some people feel guilty if they have money; some feel greedy if they want it. Exploring beliefs about money and what it symbolizes tells us about our values.

Examine your *assumptions* about money:

Assumptions of scarcity: "With inflation, money is not worth much." "There are no solutions to money problems."

How does not having enough money make you feel?

How does having money make you feel?

Examine your *beliefs* about money. "If I had money, I could do/be anything I wanted." "It's wicked to waste money." "I better not buy that." ("I'm not worth it" or "Another Great Depression could happen again . . .").

Without judging, for one week record your feelings, beliefs, and assumptions about money—the ways you spend, use, count, give away, waste or save money. What does money represent to you? (Power, safety, choice of lifestyle, freedom, etc.)

Assumptions of scarcity or abundance can ruin our lives. Childhood scars of poverty can produce a penny-pinching, millionaire or a spendthrift who dies penniless.

Your actions will tell you what you value. Each day write:

- What I did today that I enjoyed
- What I did today that I didn't enjoy
- What I put off doing that should have been done
- What I would have liked to have done but didn't
- What happened today that made me feel good
- What happened today that made me feel bad

Analyze your journals until you can find some common denominator—repeated themes that run through your writing. ("Today I studied when I would have preferred to socialize. I value a degree, future success, and an education.")

Clarifying our values can give us direction in our lives. Ask yourself, "How would I live if I knew I was going to die in one year"? "If my house burns down and everyone gets out but I only have time to save one thing, what would I save?"

Part 1: Creating Meaning

Write journal answers to the following:

- A friend is bringing a stranger to meet you. What do you want that person to notice about you? What else?

- The friend and the stranger are coming to your house. What do you want that person to notice about your house? Your lifestyle? What else?

- List three things you want to do for yourself and then do them.

- List three things you might do for someone you care about. Choose one and do it.

- Make a list of five things you prefer to do alone.

- List five things you prefer to do with others. Name those others and which items you prefer to do with them.

- Make a list of ten things in life you love to do. Rank them from most to least important. How often do you do the most important things?

- Separate the list into: 1) things that cost less than five dollars;
  2) things that cost less than twenty-five dollars;
  3) things that cost more than twenty-five dollars.

- Which items require planning? Which ones take time and energy? How do you schedule in the things you want to do?

Value Inventories

Most counseling centers have inventories to help people find out what they value. One classifies values into six categories:

Theory: The person who values theory values the discovery of "truth." Such people characteristically take a cognitive attitude. Their interests are empirical, critical, rational, intellectual. Their chief aim is to order their knowledge like the scientist or philosopher.

Economics: The person who values economics is interested in what is practical. Based originally upon self-preservation, economic needs today result in attention to business (production, marketing, consumption of goods, credit, accumulation). Practical people want a useful education and their knowledge to be applied in some concrete way.

Aesthetics: The person who values aesthetics sees highest value in form and harmony. Such people judge experience from the standpoint of grace, symmetry or fitness. "To make a thing charming is a million times more important than to make it true." They find interest in art and tend toward individualism and self-sufficiency.

Social: The social person values human beings and the altruistic aspects of love for people. Such people prize others as ends. They tend to be kind, sympathetic, and fulfilled through human relations.

Politics: The political person is primarily interested in power. Such people like to lead, to make decisions, to influence others, to gain renown. Often they enjoy competition and struggle.

Religion: The religious person values the mystical, the cosmos, unity, absolutes, divinity. Such people may prefer to withdraw from life and meditate.

This classification of values—theory, economics, aesthetics, social, political, and religious—is just one of the many systems you might like to look at, think about, and consider in your study and choice of personal guidelines. Rate yourself on each of these six categories using a scale from 0 (none) to 10 (highest).

ORDERING VALUES

From each of the following lists, pick out the one value you consider most important. On a separate piece of paper write that value on line 1. Then choose the value which is second most important. Write it on line 2. Do the same for each of the remaining values for both of these two scales:

- States of Existence

    1. Comfort (prosperity)
    2. Excitement (stimulation, activity)
    3. Accomplishment (lasting contribution)
    4. Beauty (nature and the arts)
    5. Equality (brotherhood, justice)
    6. Family ties (caring for loved ones)
    7. Freedom (independence, free choice)
    8. Happiness (contentment)
    9. Inner harmony (freedom from inner conflict)
    10. Love (sexual and spiritual intimacy)
    11. Pleasure (enjoyment, leisure)
    12. Self-respect (self-esteem)
    13. Friendship (companionshp)
    14. Wisdom (understanding life)
    15. Recognition (respect, admiration)

- Behavior

    1. Ambitious (hardworking, aspiring)
    2. Broad-minded (open-minded)
    3. Capable (competent, effective)
    4. Cheerful (lighthearted, joyful)
    5. Clean, (neat, tidy)
    6. Courageous (stand up for beliefs)
    7. Helpful (to others)
    8. Honest (sincere, truthful)
    9. Imaginative (creative)
    10. Independent (self-sufficient)
    11. Intellectual (intelligent)
    12. Loving (affectionate, caring)
    13. Responsible (dependable, reliable)
    14. Self-controlled (self-disciplined)
    15. Logical (consistent, rational)

Values in Transition

Each of us is constantly in transition. As we grow and change, our values change. Once we achieve financial security, many of us no longer care about accumulating money. After working for twenty years, we may value leisure time. By reassessing our changing values, we can avoid getting stuck in the past.

Become aware of your personal transitions.

- What did you want for Christmas when you were five years old?

- What did you want for Christmas when you were ten years old?

- What happened to many of the things you worked hard to get?

- What things did you want five years ago that you no longer value?

- What relationships did you have in the past that no longer work for you?

Once we achieve what we want, we often move on to wanting what we don't have. This movement is part of personal change and growth.

Humans have few survival needs other than food, water, and shelter. Babies need care and touch, but there is no research that finds adults have a personal survival need for sex, reproduction, or love. We tell ourselves we "need" these things because we are programmed to believe that we do. To avoid self-deception, change expressions like "I need you" to "I want to spend time (the rest of my life?) with you". People who manipulate others say, "I need you" as if they can't live without the other person. Such statements are unconscious attempts to force others to accept responsibility for their happiness. Needy people drive others away. Each of us is responsible for what we want and for creating satisfaction in our own lives without using others as need-satisfying objects.

Decision-Making

Our lives are deeply affected by the decisions we make. If we know what we value, decision-making becomes easier. Yet few of us are aware of what influences our decisions. A whole generation of children who lived through the Great Depression of 1929 were traumatized when their fathers lost their jobs. Many families lost everything—houses, furniture, cars. Financial security directed future decision-making. Couples worked hard, lived frugally, saved their money, bought houses, and *never* bought anything on credit. Their children, who grew up with financial security, lived after World War II, with the atomic bomb and the possibility that the world might end at any time. The postwar baby boomers valued "living in the here and now". Affluent baby boomer's tended to overload their own children with possessions bought on credit. As these children try to keep up with their peer group—consumerism, conspicuous consumption, and personal debt will balloon. These transformations through three generations illustrate how values and decisions change to fit the historical context and changing values of our lives.

Today diversity in lifestyles includes being married, staying single, heterosexual or homosexual relationships, having or not having children. Divorce, unacceptable in earlier times, now occurs in half of all marriages. Many divorced people remarry, creating blended families of "his, hers, and ours." Workers not only change jobs and professions often but can, if necessary, live on welfare, unemployment, social security, and other social welfare programs that did not exist in the past.

Freedom to choose isn't free, however. Each lifestyle comes with its price. Stress, anxiety, confusion or even depression accompany free choice. When faced with a choice, many people lose touch with what they value, what is important to them, and how they want to order their priorities. Decisions often involve inner conflict. Is it worthwhile to give up a vacation in Hawaii to save more money for a house? We have to give up one thing in order to get another, yet we seldom have any satisfactory procedure for weighing costs and benefits.

Not making a decision is a decision not to choose. We make or avoid making decisions every day—some so routine like brushing teeth that we hardly think about them. Some decisions take a long time while others can be decided almost instantly.

Below is a list of decisions. After each item write down whether you could make a decision in a minute or less, five minutes, an hour, a day, a month, or over a long period of time.

- What to eat
- Whether to marry
- What time to go to bed
- Whether to change jobs

- What kind of car to buy
- What to spend money on
- What clothes to wear
- Whether to get a college degree
- Which movie to see
- When to go to work
- Whether to have children

Some of these decisions are made daily while others are made only once.

Some very important decisions are surprisingly easy to make. Automatic or routine habits often save us time.
Examples from journals:

> *What I eat is not important to me. I can order in two minutes. I eat a variety of foods from the four basic food groups. I eat to live, not live to eat.*

> *I get anxious trying to decide what to wear to work. So I rotate what I wear—one outfit for each day of the week. It saves me time and eliminates anxiety.*

Some decisions such as education, housing, and marriage usually require thought and planning. Although some people are impulse buyers or marry someone shortly after they meet, most people take time to make important decisions. If they want to buy a house or car that they can't afford, they plan, get information, start a savings account and develop a line of credit.

Decisions for the most complex life situations are often difficult because we can never find out all the facts. Taking marriage and family classes to learn what it would be like to be married is no guarantee that a marriage will last. Although there are no guarantees that any decision will be a good one, certain individuals seem to be better decision-makers than others.
Examples from journals:

> *I don't remember making a decision to go to college. I remember when I was about eight or nine years old, my aunt said, "When you go to college, I'm going to buy you a white convertible with red leather seats . . .". I just assumed that I was going to college.*

> *I spent four years with one man before I decided to marry him. I made a list of reasons why I should marry him and reasons why I shouldn't—a list of his strengths and weaknesses. After twenty years, the lists are the same.*

Becoming aware of how you make decisions may help you improve your decision-making skills. When faced with a decision do you—usually, sometimes, or seldom:

- Feel nervous and anxious
- Think about what the result might be
- Put it off
- Ask others what they think
- Make the decision based on intuition rather than information
- Choose the first or second thing you think of
- Feel confident that you can make a good one
- Think through and plan

Write specific examples and analyze the results.

Certain decision-making habits are self-defeating. Individuals who habitually procrastinate often put off making decisions until it is too late and they lose opportunities to achieve their goals. Those unwilling to be responsible for making decisions wait until someone else tells them what to do. Then if the decision doesn't work, they blame others—a tactic that never works. Some individuals leave decisions to chance by simply not deciding. Others choose the first thing that comes to mind rather than getting information about the best way to do something. Evaluate how you make decisions. Be aware of self-deception.

Give an example of a decision you avoided:

- You procrastinated too long

- You let others make the decision

- You did not decide

- You took the easy way out

What was the final result?

- Do you use a variety of decision-making techniques depending upon the importance of the decision and situation? Give an example.

- Write an example of when you made a bad decision.

I made an investment that I didn't sell soon enough. I should have read up on what was going on instead of ignoring it as I have a tendency to do.

I chose to graduate from college in four years. I was dependent upon my parents. Today I would extend my college career and work so I would have job experience on my resume.

I went to school in L.A. to get away from home. Everything there was a disappointment—too trendy and too fake. I wish I had gone to college here at home with my friends.

I made a mistake choosing my career. If I could do it again, I would choose work with more economic benefits. I like what I do, but there are lots of things I like doing.

I've made wrong decisions in relationships. I seem unable to find someone compatible. I don't seem to find the trust and mutual respect I am looking for. The separations are inevitable.

Getting married. I was too young. I didn't think of the commitment and how much I would have to give up.

Every decision can't be a good one. You may be excellent in making financial decisions, yet a failure at making decisions about relationships. You can learn from decisions that do not work.

If you decide to change unproductive habits, you can learn to replace them with more productive ones. If you are satisfied with your life, you will have no desire to change; but if you are dissatisfied, you can learn new behaviors. Professional planners follow these steps:

1. Identify the decision
2. Explore alternatives
3. Gather information
4. Predict outcomes
5. Design a plan of action
6. Implement the plan

You can learn and use this decision-making process. Follow the example given step by step. Then apply the process to a personal decision you want to make.

- First—identify a decision

    My car won't start. It needs one thousand dollars worth of repairs. I have to decide how to provide myself with transportation.

- Second—explore alternatives
    1. Take the bus
    2. Buy another car
    3. Walk
    4. Borrow a car
    5. Car pool to work
    6. Ride a bike
    7. Have my car fixed
    8. Try to find someone who works on cars
    9. Buy the parts at an auto supply store
    10. Sell my nonoperable car

- Third—gather information about the alternatives
    1. Get a bus schedule, bus route, bus fare
    2. Read the want ads, visit an auto dealer, get prices
    3. I can eliminate walking because the distance is too far
    4. I don't want the responsibility of using someone else's car

5. Put an ad in the paper to car pool, put a sign up at work, check with personnel to find out who lives near me
6. I don't have a bike and don't want to buy one
7. Get more information on my car, compare estimates from repair shops

Some alternatives immediately eliminate themselves. For example, I don't have one thousand dollars and can't borrow it; the alternative to have my car fixed therefore eliminates itself. We may eliminate a few good alternatives, but usually we end up with a few of the best ones.

- Fourth—predict outcomes
    1. The bus will take more time than I want to waste.
       I could read and relax on the bus.
    2. I can't qualify for credit to buy a new car.
    3. If I find someone to car pool to work, I might meet a new group of people. But I still won't have transportation other than to and from work.
    4. Nonoperating cars sell for about fifty dollars. I will lose too much money.
    5. If I buy all the parts at an auto supply store and someone helps me fix my car, it still might not work.
- Fifth—design a plan of action (Complete these statements:)
    1. I am going to take the following action

    2. I will start on (day)

    3. I will take the following steps

4. I could have these kinds of problems

5. I can try this alternate plan

6. Sixth—take action

Begin on the date you stated in your plan of action. Write your progress from beginning to end. Sometimes you may use two or more of your alternatives or a combination of alternatives.

This decision-making process becomes automatic for people who use it often. However, not every decision in life can be made by thinking and planning. Some people have hunches and act on them successfully. Others make decisions based on their feelings about something or someone. Because their decisions work, they come to trust their intuitions or their feelings.

Assuming that you make decisions using both head and heart:

- Do you depend more on intuition or on reasoning?

- Describe examples of decisions you have made.

- Make a list of decisions that have worked best.

- Make a list of decisions that didn't work.

Analyze these two lists. What made the difference?

Important information in life comes through elimination—learning what doesn't work. Most college students change their majors after getting more information at least three times before they graduate. Working at a job can teach us that we are not suited for that field. We can also learn from relationships that end. A wise person asks: "What have I learned from this experience"? We change jobs, friends, houses, or mates. We base decisions on the information we have at the time we make them. After a decision is made, we get more information. A decision that works at one point in life may not work at another time.

Irreversible Decisions

Although at times you *pretend* to yourself that every major decision is a matter of life or death, you can always choose what to do about the consequences. You can make new decisions. You can decide to quit or go back to school, to change jobs or sell a house, to begin or end a marriage. No matter how wise you are, as a growing, changing person some past choices are no longer appropriate today. Both you and your values change.

A missed opportunity will be replaced by some other experience, and you can never be sure the missed opportunity would have worked out better. Given all the information you had at a given time, considering the person you were and the situation you were in, you probably made the best decision at that moment.

The next time you will have more information to make another decision.

Irreversible decisions—where nothing *further can be done—are rare. However, many decisions have lifelong effects.*

- Make a list of decisions that might have lifelong effects.

- List alternatives for each of these.

Every choice has its price. One attitude you can choose is that we do not make mistakes, we simply make choices. Some work, others don't, and we have to live with the consequences.

Making good decisions builds self-confidence. Although the decisions you must make are infinite and never-ending, you can order priorities and improve your decision-making.

Marking Transitions

Many cultures have rituals that celebrate the transformation from one stage of life to the next. These rites provide experiences that record life changes, mark passages, and celebrate births, graduations, and marriages. Crises occur in most families—alcoholism, drug addiction, a terminal illness—which have a profound affect on our lives. These crises force us to cope with our transitions. It is important to note these passages, to know when we've passed through a particular door.

Write on the following:

- When I got my driver's license

- When I left home

- When I could vote

- When I got married

- When my first child was born

Make your own list of critical or significant events in your life.

JOURNAL EXAMPLE

I experienced a period of depression for which I could find no cause. I woke up on the morning of my birthday. A thought flashed through my mind: "I made it!". I was one year older than the age at which my father died. I had outlived him and this transformation unconsciously affected me. With this insight, my depression lifted.

Life is a process. We are continually in transition, yet at any given moment we are unaware of the many changes that occur. We can mark these mysterious passages into and out of life stages by acknowledging transformation and change. Thoreau said: "Every man tracks himself through life". Each of us in our thinking, feeling, and observing follows our own footprints on this earth. In this journal you have been recording some of your life as others have recorded the history of civilizations.

Part Two

Aspects of Communication

Communication is so complex that it is difficult to control. Yet expanding awareness of the process can lead to more effective communication. Intrapersonal communication is communicating with the self. Writing is a form of communicating with the self in a way that makes what is going on inside of us more tangible. We can look at what we have written. And often we can then find the truth of ourselves. The activities in this section of the journal can help you experience parts of yourself in concrete ways.

Part Two of the journal investigates body, emotions, language, thoughts, and actions—all ways in which we communicate, whether we are conscious of them or not. Communication is more than language. It is impossible to be alive and *not* communicate. Words you think, emotions you feel, actions you take even without thinking are forms of communication. When you experience an emotion, your body responds. It communicates to you. Your body communicates meaning to you and to others simply in the way you walk and the way you stand.

Communication involves our environment, other people, and ourselves. *Everything communicates.* Communication is continuous: it comes from the past, occurs now, moves into the future. Communication is irreversible: if you say something, you can never take it back. You can add to it, but added remarks only continue the process; they do not erase or reverse it. In the following chapters we will go beyond word language to what we think, what our body communicates, what we feel, and what we do—all interrelated aspects of communication.

Knowing is a translation of external events into bodily processes . . . into states of the nervous system and the brain: we know the world in terms of the body, and in accordance with its structure.
Alan Watts

5

How the Body Communicates

Actors, dancers, opera singers, and other professionals consciously use gestures, facial expressions, posture, and gait to communicate. Many people who choose to remain expressionless intend not to communicate nonverbally. Part of their identity is to hide emotions, thoughts, responses. You can choose to communicate nonverbally. And you can choose to expand your awareness of all your senses. You can extend your awareness out into your environment. You can use your body as a vehicle for communication. These choices are yours.

By expanding your consciousness of the nonverbal communication of others, you can enrich your relationships as you expand your knowledge of others. You can become perceptive enough to nonverbal communication to pick up muscle twitches and eyeblinks, change in skin color, and increases in breathing rate. At other times you may become so concerned with your own thoughts and responses that you miss these nonverbal clues. The intention of this chapter is to increase your capacity to send and receive nonverbal communication.

NONVERBAL COMMUNICATION

Tapping feet, drumming fingers, pen clicking—all these mannerisms may indicate boredom, nervousness, or simply habit. Avoiding a look may be interpreted as dishonesty or shyness. Yet both these interpretations could be wrong. The problem is that many of us do not know *what* we are doing with our faces, hands, feet, or bodies. And, in addition, we often do not know what it means when we do become aware of these movements.

Students in a communication class made a list of gestures, body movements, facial expressions, sounds, and other nonverbal signals. Then they made a column for what these signals might signify—there were close to ten different meanings for each item listed. Then they discussed how these signals made them feel. The feelings were as varied as the number of students in the class. They discussed making involuntary sounds (a sigh, a groan, a giggle) or taking a deep breath. They talked about laughing. A laugh may indicate humor, embarrassment, anxiety, or fear. The person who laughs doesn't always know what it means because it is sometimes involuntary. One student wrote: "I never stopped before to notice or think about nonverbal communication, gestures, or body movements. Now that I have, I see so much more. At times I can even see what my own face is doing. It's very exciting to be more conscious."

ASPECTS OF NONVERBAL COMMUNICATION

Reflecting on the following nonverbal aspects of communication will help you become more aware of ways other than language by which we communicate.

- Choose items from the list and write a detailed description of yourself. Write about your best friend in terms of some of these aspects of nonverbal communication. Then look at the selection of items you chose. What do your choices tell you about yourself?

    Physical characteristics: height, weight, gender, skin color, size of nose, color of eyes

    Body structure: build, bone size, posture (erect, bent), chest position, shoulders, arms, legs

    Facial expressions: mouth (smiles, grimaces, muscle movements); nose (nostrils flared/pinched); eyes (contact, avoidance, pupil dilation); forehead or jaw (tense/relaxed)

    Walk: distinctions (stride, pace, strut)

    Touch: hand shake (grip, hold), back slapping, punching, pulling, holding, caressing

    Gestures: using hands, arms, head, legs, body

    Voice: pitch, tone, rhythm, stress, volume, expression (angry, humble, sad, happy)

    Appearance: dress, grooming, scent

    Environmental factors: living space, working space, colors, arrangement of furniture

Time/space: atmosphere, personal space/distance, territory, seating arrangement

Social influences: class, church, business, family context, large group, small group, one to one, privacy

Cultural differences: distancing, odors, privacy/space

Physical condition: tired, in pain, energetic, healthy

Emotions: fear, anxiety, trust, defensiveness, joy

- Set up your own research experiments. Notice how people use their eyes. See if you can hold eye contact with others as you pass them on the street. Notice what people do with their eyes and bodies in an elevator, while standing in line, while shopping in a store. Write about your findings. Create your own experiments on any of the items listed here:

  1. Winking
  2. Blinking
  3. Tapping feet
  4. Drumming fingers
  5. Scratching hair or face
  6. Shaking foot or leg
  7. Pulling or playing with hair
  8. Licking or biting lips
  9. Shaking head
  10. Chewing hands or pencil
  11. Tapping teeth
  12. Sticking out tongue
  13. Tapping pen or pencil
  14. Staring
  15. Shaking fist or finger
  16. Cracking knuckles
  17. Clicking pen
  18. Frowning
  19. Snapping fingers
  20. Rubbing nose
  21. Avoiding eye contact
  22. Others

- Make a list of nonverbal expressions communicating warmth/coldness. For example: tone of voice (soft/hard); body (relaxed/tense); gestures (expressive/guarded).

- Write the name of another person and a description of the way that person expresses himself or herself (eyes, face, chin, and so on).

86   Part 2: Aspects of Communication

- Write whatever else you notice about the faces, bodies, postures, and structures of others. Who has most of his or her weight in the top part of the body? How does that person balance the weight (forward, backward, centered)?

- Write a description of yourself: facial expressions, use of eyes, jaw, nostrils, muscles, body structure, and so forth.

BEYOND PHYSICAL ATTRACTIVENESS

Once we are aware of our culturally programmed biases about physical attractiveness, we begin to note how they affect our judgment of others.

- How do you feel about physical attractiveness? What kind of person do you think is physically attractive? Describe the qualities (hair, teeth, skin) you find attractive.

- Write a description of your own body. Do you consider yourself attractive? How do you feel about your physical structure (height, weight, shape)?

- Do you consider yourself healthy? How does your health affect your attractiveness?

- What are your physical abilities (sports, dancing, manual dexterity)?

- What do you dislike about your body? What do you like about your face (eyes, mouth, neck, teeth)? What features do you dislike?

- Write about some of the disadvantages of being considered attractive in our culture.

- What does your body tell you about yourself? Your posture? Your facial features? The way you move and walk?

- What attitudes do you have about bodies? What images get in the way of your relationship with yourself and others?

UNSPOKEN MESSAGES

We are often unaware of how clothes and body impressions communicate.

- Write about clothing messages:

    1. Whose clothes have you noticed today (including jewelry)?

    2. What do you think clothing says about that person?

    3. What do you want your clothes to say about you?

    4. What do others think your clothing says about you?

5. What values do you place on clothes? What effect do clothes have on a viewer today?

6. List five items of clothing you notice.

- Write about body impressions:
    1. What is the first thing you notice about another person?

    2. What part of a person's body do you look at first?

    3. What part of a man's body do you look at first? A woman's body? Number the parts you look at in order: 1, 2, 3, and so on.

VOCALIZATION

There are many different elements of vocalization. Think about them, and describe them without making any judgments.

- Describe your voice qualities: pitch range, pitch control, rhythm, tempo, articulation, resonance.

- Vocal characteristics include laughing, crying, sighing, yawning, belching, coughing, whispering. For the next few days observe vocal characteristics (both your own and others). Write about what you have noticed.

- Notice when you use speech pauses ("um," "uh," "ah"). Notice when others use them. Write about someone who uses them a great deal. How does a person who uses speech pauses create a different message (or identity) than a person who rarely uses speech pauses?

- Listen to your own voice. How does it sound? What is your emotional reaction to your own voice?

RULES ABOUT TOUCHING

Touching is intimately tied to each culture. Studies show that Greeks and Arabs are the most contact-oriented while Scottish women are the least touchable. Moreover, differences occur in families with different religious training. Professions have different unwritten rules about touching also. Nurses, for example, are more likely to touch younger patients than older ones. Children, in all situations, are touched more often than teenagers.

In every culture these "rules," although unspoken, set the limits for appropriateness of touch depending on the situation and those involved. Dr. Richard Heslin at Purdue has classified touching in our culture as functional/professional; social/polite; friendship/warmth; or love/intimacy.

In the *functional/professional* relationship, a person is touched as an object in order for the toucher to do something to the receiver. The doctor/patient, fireman/victim, barber/customer touching relationship is restricted to a businesslike manner. Touch to be appropriate must be "cold and unsympathetic."

In the *social/polite* relationship, unwritten rules allow touching under strict cultural restraint. The handshake or the kiss on the cheek, depending on the culture, acknowledges that two persons are on equal footing—not friends but not enemies.

In the *friendship/warmth* relationship, touching is less formalized; therefore it can cause the most uneasiness because it might be misinterpreted as love or sexual attraction. Touching is especially threatening with the same sex. Threatening feelings are greater when the friendship/warmth touching takes place in privacy because privacy is associated with sex.

In the *love/intimacy* relationship, touching gets complicated by childhood background and experiences. Religious training can cause problems. One style of touch may be defined as "masculine" as opposed to tender touching. Different areas of the body may respond differently. Touching hands and face may imply safety to one person and threat to another. Touching genitals has a highly sexual component. For some people, a touch that conveys sexual desire may not convey love. For others, the two are combined. Playful touching, pleasant touching, loving touching, and sexual desire often get confused.

Even married couples have trouble communicating through touch. Often they are confused about what they want and what they intend by touching. One study showed that while wives believed they were expressing positive feelings, husbands often felt threatened by touch. The study showed that when a man is feeling low, a sexual touch can cause even greater anxiety about his masculinity, especially when the wife inititates the touching. The subject has no end of complexities which, when even partially understood, can contribute much to improved intra/interpersonal relations.

ON TOUCHING

This activity will help you recall how your attitudes toward touching from the past have affected your current behavior.

- What is your first memory of touching and being touched?

- Who else was important in your experiences of touching and being touched?

- Explain your present values and feelings about touching and being touched. For example: Do I want to be touched? (How and under what conditions?) Do I want to tcuch? (How and under what conditions?)

- Are you satisfied with these feelings and values?

PHYSICAL AGGRESSION

There is a fine line between hitting in a playful or teasing way and hitting with the intent to hurt. Becoming more conscious of our intentions can improve our relating and communicating.

- Write about an experience of hitting someone or being hit.

- Do you fear a physical fight?
- Where do you draw your personal line between physical playing and hurting?
- What were the family rules about hitting and fighting when you were a child?
- What family rules about hitting and fighting would you want for your children?

BODY WORK

Body work can communicate to you through the physical sensations. Physical behavior is predominantly nonverbal and usually operates without awareness. A sunken chest cage, when expanded, brings a natural sense of self-assertion; tight muscles in the face or neck speak their own messages. No explanations are needed once you become aware of your habits. Any distortions will correct themselves when they have been experienced and brought to consciousness. In the use of motion and breathing, notice if your muscles are rigid and controlled or flabby and unstructured. Notice whether you are tense or inert. Move toward centering if either of these two extremes is your habitual pattern. Here are some exercises to get you in touch with your body:

1. Stand up and tense every muscle in your body. Begin with those in your head and neck and move downward. Hold the tension for a few moments and then begin relaxing each muscle from your toes upward.

2. Notice how tension affects you. Notice how the releasing of it feels.

3. Sit down, close your eyes, and with your fingertips begin tapping your head in a steady rhythm moving all over and around. Concentrate on the feeling of aliveness.

4. Breathing: Close your eyes and sit in a comfortable position. Take some time to get in touch with your body. Now focus your attention on your breathing. Notice as the air flows effortlessly in and out. Feel the air as it moves into your nose or mouth. Feel it as it goes down your throat into your chest. Let your belly expand and receive this life-giving air. Imagine a surge of energy filling you. Now imagine that you breathe into other body parts: into your pelvis, down your legs, into your toes; into your arms and fingers; into your head and neck.

5. Yawning: Take a deep breath. Open your mouth wide into a full yawn. Let the air out.

HANDLING STRESS

How we handle stress is intimately related to our personalities.

- In the process of becoming aware of stress, notice in yourself or others the following: withdrawal, shyness, talkativeness, acting distant or snobbish, clenching teeth, averting eyes, tensing muscles. What are your characteristic stress reactions? What provokes stress in you?

- Begin to notice different degrees of tension in yourself. Describe three situations that provoke different levels of stress for you.

- Getting in touch with your stress level involves recognizing body signals. What are your characteristic body signals for positive stress? Negative stress?

- Write about three situations in which you felt too much stress and how it affected your behavior.

- Write about three situations in which you did not feel enough stress and as a result did not perform as well as you could have.

REDUCING STRESS

Many techniques have been developed for stress reduction. Here are three that can be practiced ten to fifteen minutes a day.

- *Progressive relaxation:* Find a quiet place out of doors. Also find a quiet mental space. Put aside matters not conducive to relaxation. Now make yourself comfortable and close your eyes. Next take a long, slow, deep breath and let it go. Become aware of the difference between tension and relaxation by tensing a muscle and then letting it go. Start with your hands. Make a fist and tighten it. Then tighten your wrists. Hold these muscles tight for a count of twenty and then let them go. They should tremble. Then tighten your forehead, face, and mouth. Hold for ten seconds and let go. Arch your back, raise your chest, push your shoulders back as hard as you can. Hold for a count of ten then relax. Now tighten your stomach, hold for a count of ten and relax. Tighten all your leg muscles, starting with your toes and working up to your thighs. Hold and relax. Relaxation requires a letting go without effort, will, or plan.

- *Autosuggestion:* Program your biocomputer by giving yourself suggestions. Make yourself comfortable; close your eyes; take a long, slow, deep breath and let it go. Get rid of all body tension. Inhale slowly and deeply. Pause a moment. Then exhale slowly and completely. Do this several times. Tell yourself: "I now feel calm, comfortable, and more relaxed than before. My feet feel heavy. My ankles and lower legs are relaxed. My stomach, pelvis, and back are relaxed. My shoulders, neck, jaw, mouth, and eyes are relaxed." Now just rest and allow your whole body to relax. With each breath you let out you will relax a little more. You are now in a calm, relaxed state. You can deepen this state by counting backward. Breathe in. As you exhale slowly, say to yourself: "Ten, I am feeling very relaxed." Inhale and say: "Nine, I am feeling more relaxed." "Eight, I am feeling even more relaxed than before." Continue . . . three . . . two . . . one . . . zero. "I am now at a deep, relaxed, peaceful level. I can stay in this relaxed state as long as I choose. Each time I relax like this I will find it easier and easier to relax more deeply until I will relax deeply just by breathing in and out and allowing myself to let go."

- *Imagery:* In the chapter on the mind, we will read about visualization and imagery. Here is one example of how imagery can be used to reduce stress. Find a tranquil place. Get into a comfortable position, close your eyes, and breathe slowly until you feel very relaxed. Take about five minutes to empty your mind and relax all your muscles. Now you are in a calm, relaxed state. *Imagine* yourself in an elevator. Watch the doors close. Now look at the panel above the door and imagine number 10 is lit up. Feel the motion as the elevator begins to descend. As the elevator slowly passes each floor you will become more and more relaxed. Now see the numbers . . . 9 . . . 8 . . . 7 . . . continue counting as you feel more relaxed . . . 3 . . . 2 . . . 1. You are now in a deep, relaxed state. See the elevator doors open. Walk out into a small, comfortable room that is dimly lit. On the wall in front of you is a large screen. Facing the screen is a chair. Sit comfortably, deeply relaxed. Now allow images to come on the screen. Stay in this relaxed space as long as you wish. When you want to return, enter the elevator and return to the tenth floor feeling rested, strong, and relaxed.

DEALING WITH SPACE

This activity will help you become more aware of how we set up boundaries and use distance to separate ourselves from others.

- In a conversation, move closer (little by little) to another person. Notice any discomfort or movement by the other person. Write about this experiment.

- In a large room or auditorium where there are many seats, go sit by another person . . . in the next seat. Notice any response and write about it. Repeat this experiment a number of times and see if you can come to any conclusions.

- Objects such as clothes, jewelry, glasses, cars, furniture, and other possessions convey nonverbal messages. Belongings also have "territories" or space boundaries. Create your own experiments and write about objects in relation to space boundaries.

Man is the only animal that laughs and weeps; for he is the only animal that is struck by the difference between what things are and what they might have been.

William Hazlitt

6

How Feelings Communicate

Psychologists and philosophers often suggest that *supposedly* negative emotions contribute to our awareness and growth. Feeling and expressing anger, fear, depression, loneliness, boredom, and ambivalence can be extremely difficult in our culture because we have often been told "Don't feel bad. Everything will be okay." As a result, the communication of emotions is often avoided. When we pretend we do not feel something that we do feel, we soon lose touch with our feelings.

D. H. Lawrence said: "We can go wrong in our minds, but what our blood feels and believes and says is always true." Feelings are natural and they can be constructive. The skilled expression of feelings must be learned, however. Certain skills of communicating emotions can enrich both self-awareness and relationships with others.

Sources of difficulty in communicating feelings are complex. First our language is limited. But more important is the fact that we are often not aware of our feelings. Moreover, cultural prohibitions sometimes restrict people who feel embarrassed either at expressing feelings or having others express them. And in relationships, feelings may be interpreted as manipulation, demand, or obligation. Some people have trouble recognizing and accepting feelings. The intent of this chapter is to integrate your feelings into the whole system of communicating.

PROGRAMMED EMOTIONAL RESPONSES

Every culture has certain unwritten rules about appropriate feelings to fit certain situations. Yet people react in unique ways because feelings are very personal. Students asked to remember incidents when their feelings did not fit expectations (either their own or someone else's) listed the following examples:

"I didn't cry when my grandmother died. My parents were very upset. I began to wonder if something was wrong with me."

"I didn't cry when I left home. I was excited about going to live in a new country with new people. My mother couldn't understand why I didn't feel sad. So I felt guilty about being excited."

"A cop arrested me. I broke out laughing. He really got mad."

"I laughed when I hurt myself and my friend thought I was crazy."

"When my mother said 'Pack your clothes and get out,' I felt glad. She got all upset and said she needed me."

"When my father slapped me, I hit him back. I didn't feel guilty or bad. I felt really good."

"My mother came to me in tears and said, 'Your unmarried cousin is going to have a baby.' I said 'So what?' My mother got mad and gave me a big speech about responsibility, but I don't have any feelings about it."

"I cry when I experience something beautiful like a new baby or a wedding. My boyfriend thinks I'm crazy."

APPROPRIATE FEELINGS

This activity can help you explore programmed feelings so that you can choose appropriate emotional responses.

- Make a list of sayings that are passed on from generation to generation telling us how we should or should not feel. For example: "You shouldn't be angry" "You shouldn't cry." "Don't be afraid! That's silly."

- Describe a time when you felt guilty because you did not feel a feeling that you thought was appropriate for that situation. How did others respond to you?

- Write about a time when you told someone that he or she should (or should not) feel his or her feelings.

- Recall a time when you tried to tell yourself that you should or should not feel your feelings.

- Write about a time when you responded in an unexpected way and someone was bothered by your response. Write about a time when someone else responded in a way that you felt was inappropriate.

In our culture, we have been programmed to believe that we ought to be happy—that if we are unhappy we are neurotic or need help. Many of us are eager to help others solve their problems. We love giving advice and take great pleasure in acting out the role of counselor or psychologist. Do-it-yourself therapy books sell by the millions. They deny that it is all right, at times, to be unhappy.

It is in fact human, at times, to feel depressed, anxious, angry, and discontented. Almost every human being has experienced failure, being unable to achieve a goal, unrealized expectations. Differences of opinion and unpleasantness in relationships are sometimes unavoidable and may even be outright positive occurrences that are required for growth. We do not need to be content all the time. And we do not need to apologize or rationalize our unhappy feelings. And we do not need to rush out and help our loved ones "solve" their problems or resolve their unpleasant feelings. What each of us does need is the experience that painful feelings will pass, that some things simply take time to work out, that not everything needs to be explained, and that pain often results in personal growth.

Although we may want to understand, there is a good deal about others and even about ourselves that we will *never* understand. We can expect that each of us is often irrational, inconsistent, childish, even unfair. We can learn that the "why" is less important than the effort to keep others from suffering because of us. But if they choose to experience pain, then they too are free to create their own experiences. When we spend less energy on trying to be happy, we discover the internal resources to grow through all our emotional experiences.

THE VOCABULARY OF EMOTIONS

We need words, a vocabulary list, to express the nuances in our feelings, emotions, and moods. Here are two such vocabularies, one negative and one positive:

Negative List		Positive List	
abandoned	defeated	accepted	desirable
alienated	degraded	adequate	determined
ambivalent	depressed	affectionate	ecstatic
angry	destructive	alive	empathetic
annoyed	dishonest	aware	energetic
anxious	distracted	brave	excited
apathetic	disturbed	calm	fascinated
betrayed	embarrassed	capable	flexible
bitter	empty	cheerful	free
bored	envious	clever	friendly
childish	foolish	committed	generous
compulsive	frantic	confident	gentle
condemned	frustrated	contented	glad
confused	guilty	cooperative	good
deceitful	gullible	delighted	good-looking

Negative List		*Positive List*	
hated	outraged	happy	proud
helpless	persecuted	helpful	relaxed
hopeless	pressured	high	rewarded
hostile	rebellious	honored	solemn
hurt	rejected	humorous	spontaneous
ignored	restless	inspired	sympathetic
impotent	sad	involved	tranquil
inadequate	scared	joyous	trusted
inferior	skeptical	kind	trusting
intimidated	spiteful	loving	understood
jealous	tense	mystical	unique
lazy	threatened	nice	vital
lonely	trapped	peaceful	vivacious
miserable	violent	pleasant	wonderful
obsessed	vulnerable	pleased	worthwhile

- Go through the negative vocabulary of emotions and circle those words that affect you most. Keep going through the list until you end up with the ten negative emotions you experience most often.

- Order these emotions from most often experienced to least.

- Choose several of them and write about a time when you experienced those negative feelings.
- Think about some positive results from those negative experiences. See if you can discover some new insight gained from them.
- Now circle the positive words that you experience the most. Follow the same procedure you used for negative emotions.

DEALING WITH FEELINGS

We need to explore new ways of expressing emotion so that we can communicate the feelings we intend to communicate.

- List as many sources of difficulty in communicating feelings as you can think of: language, unawareness, conflicts, and so forth.

- What are some of the cultural taboos against expression of feelings? For example: "Feelings interfere with solving problems." "Don't get carried away." "Be logical."

- What happens when you suppress feelings rather than communicate them?

- How do you express your feelings? Are some means of expression more appropriate than others (or more effective)?

- How do you handle ambivalent feelings? Can you communicate ambivalent feelings?

EXPRESSING EMOTIONS

Any single emotion is experienced differently at different times by the same person. We need to ask ourselves about the meaning of our emotions.

- Write down examples of anger, fear, depression, loneliness, boredom, and ambivalence that have contributed to your self-knowledge.

- Find examples of what famous people say about their experiences with feelings. For example:

    1. About being alone, Albert Camus said:

        *Strange; inability to be alone
        inability not to be alone.
        One accepts both.
        Both profit.*

        Thoreau said: "I find it wholesome to be alone the greater part of the time. . . . I love to be alone. I never found the companion that was so companionable as solitude."

        C. E. M. Joad felt "a perpetual alternation between two rhythms, the rhythm of attracting people for fear I may be lonely and the rhythm of trying to get rid of them because . . . I am bored."

    2. About anxiety, Woody Allen said: "Anxiety is the natural state of man, and so I think it's probably the correct state. It's probably important that we experience anxiety because it makes for the survival of the species."

- Ask yourself the meaning of these emotions for you. For example: "What is boredom? What does it feel like? What causes people to be bored?" Make a list for each emotion.

THE BENEFITS OF EMOTIONAL PAIN

Pain tells you who you are! These exercises will help you to appreciate the meaning of emotional pain.

- Take any emotional pain and list some possible benefits. For example: "Insecurity is the result of trying to be secure. Security results in the recognition that we have no way of saving ourselves."

- Recall a time when you turned fear, anxiety, insecurity, or some other pain into a positive experience.

- Recall a time when your attention to an anxious situation helped you find a solution.

- Think of positive ways anxiety and fear work for you. Give specific examples.

- When you worry, you focus your attention on a problem, which may help you to find a constructive solution. Give an example.

DESCRIBING YOUR FEELINGS

The more you put your feelings into words, the more concrete they become.

- What causes you to feel anger? Write about a time when you felt anger, frustration, or resentment. Do these three emotions all feel the same to you? Can you give examples of them and reexperience them? What do you gain when you resent someone? What do you do when you feel angry? Frustrated? Resentful?

- What are you afraid of? What do you fear most? Write about a time when you felt afraid. What did you do?

Chapter 6: How Feelings Communicate   **103**

- What makes you feel anxious? Fritz Perls says if you stay in "the here and now" you will not feel anxious. Anxiety stems from being preoccupied with the past or the future. Make a list of things you can do when you are anxious. Would you rather feel anxious or bored?

- Write about a time when getting angry (or feeling afraid or anxious) resulted in your doing something positive so that the feeling worked in some positive way.

- What makes you feel guilty? Describe a situation in which you felt guilt. Describe a time when someone tried to use guilt to manipulate you. Tell about a time you tried to make someone else feel guilty. Did it work? What was the result?

- What makes you feel jealous? Describe a time when you felt jealous. What did you do about it?

- Everyone feels depressed at some time. What depresses you? Write about a time when you felt depressed. How did the depression end?

- Write about a time when you felt lonely. How long did it last? What did you do about it? Discuss some advantage of feeling lonely.

- Write about a time you felt bored. What do you do when you're bored?

NOBODY PROMISED YOU A ROSE GARDEN

One of the most difficult feelings to handle is the feeling that you are being treated unfairly. The world is full of injustice. Hannah Green in I Never Promised You a Rose Garden *wrote: "I never promised you perfect justice . . . and I never promised you peace or happiness. . . . You can be free to fight for all these things. . . . I never promise lies, and the rose-garden world of perfection is a lie . . . and a bore, too!"*

- Write about a time when you were discriminated against and could do nothing about it. For example: because of age, sex, height, weight.

- Write about a time when you were treated unjustly. What did you do about it? What do you want to do about it now? Is it all right not to do anything? What is "righteous indignation?"

- What positive results occur with the feeling of injustice? What negative gains can occur? For example: the advantage of being able to blame an outside source for your problems.

- Is it possible to feel an emotion without acting it out? What is the relationship between feeling and behavior? Are they necessarily connected? If you accept responsibility for your feelings and you no longer wish to experience a feeling, do you have a choice about changing your attitude toward the source of the emotion? Give an example.

AMBIVALENCE AND CONFLICT

Ambivalence is the feeling of wanting something and not wanting it at the same time. A love-hate relationship where we love someone and we also feel anger toward them—or want the relationship at the same time we wish it were over—describes ambivalence. We can feel ambivalent about relationships, work, and objects.

A parent often feels ambivalent about a child; and a child often feels ambivalent about a parent. Even the mother who loves her child can, at times, resent the obligation that goes with being a mother. The feeling of joy in a relationship may be balanced, at times, by feeling angry at another person who restricts our freedom. Thus ambivalence is the coexistence of opposite feelings about the same person or object.

To exist is to be in conflict. Perhaps we must move away from a problem-solving view of life to appreciate the experience of conflict—the experience of paradoxical stress for which few can find answers. To become more successful in living is to recognize the inescapable ambiguities and contradictions in life as powerful allies. In fact contradiction can be a source of strength. To accept that conflict may not be resolved, to step back from ambivalence and look at it and experience it, to admit that contradiction may not be reconciled—all this means accepting these opposing forces as a way of knowing there are unanswerable, unsolvable issues in every life.

THE TENSION OF EXISTENCE

If you can learn to accept ambivalence and explore the tension created between inner and outer realities, you can reconcile yourself and bring order to your world.

- Write about a time when you felt ambivalent.

- Make a list of people, activities, or objects about which you have felt a positive pull and a negative feeling at the same time. What does it feel like? What do you do? How do you resolve attraction-repulsion feelings that exist at the same time?

- Make a list of opposites. For example:

    independence—dependence
    freedom—commitment
    maturity—innocence

adult—child
autonomy—subordination

- Write about a time when you experienced a need for independence and a need for dependence at the same time.

- Write about a time when you felt love and hate for the same person at the same time.

- How do you handle feeling both negative and positive about the same person at the same time?

- What person do you have mixed emotions about now?

- What feelings about yourself and others have changed in the past few years?

HIDDEN FEELINGS

There are some common patterns for hiding feelings. When people feel threatened, defensive, afraid, or rejected, they respond in certain ways. The Pleaser is afraid the other person will get angry. The Blamer is afraid of being wrong or weak or at fault. The Rationalizer is afraid of getting involved or hurt. The Distracter feels that ignoring the problem will make it go away.

Pleasers feel helpless. They think they are nothing without the other person. They feel worthless. They apologize, placate, or whine . . . anything but argue. Blamers disagree with almost everything. "You never do anything right. What's the matter with you?" Inside they are afraid. They feel lonely and unsuccessful unless they can be boss. They find fault, act superior, and cut everything and everyone else down so they can put themselves up. Rationalizers hide behind words. They act overly reasonable: "If one were to observe carefully, one might notice. . . ." They present a calm, cool, collected front. Underneath they feel vulnerable. They're afraid of feelings and may disassociate themselves from their emotions. They may use long words, complicated words, abstractions, anything rather than feel. Distracters do or say irrelevant things. They avoid contact and interaction. Inside they feel: "Nobody cares. There is no place for me." They feel terribly lonely, as if life has no purpose.

How do you react when you are trying to hide your feelings? Do any of these patterns fit you? Write examples and describe the feelings.

SEARCHING FOR HIDDEN FEELINGS

Writing works best when you do not theorize, analyze, categorize. Simply describe: recreate the experience by putting down the words you used, the thoughts in your mind, the ways your body responded, the emotions you felt, and a description of your actions.

- What did you do today? What did you feel? How did you act?

- Now go back and explore your feelings. Let the feelings flow out. Describe them; explore them. Include the physical discomfort (tension, fatigue). Keep going deeper. Try to find a feeling different from the one with which you started. Anger can cover guilt or fear or pain.

- What are you feeling now? What happened? What are you afraid to feel? What does this remind you of? What else do you feel?

- Keep going deeper and deeper. Imagine that you are peeling off one layer of emotion at a time, like layers of an onion. What's behind what you are writing now?

Self-deception covers our real feelings with other emotions. Anger may be a cover for guilt, fear, or hurt feelings. For the person who is afraid to feel angry, depression can cover anger. Perhaps you have been told: "You mustn't feel angry. That's not nice." Or "A good man controls his anger. He doesn't show it." Feeling depressed or bored can be a substitute emotion for the one we aren't supposed to feel.

Writing a journal can get you to the core emotion if you persist with the writing and dare to go deeper. You will not go any deeper than you can stand. There is a protective function in self-deception. It is a defense mechanism, and most of us will not discover anything we are not ready to look at. Yet there is an excitement about exploring the parts of one's self that have not yet been charted. Ultimately, growth comes with expanded consciousness.

Don Juan, the Indian shaman, describes the search for Carlos Casteneda:

A man goes to knowledge as he goes to war, wide awake with fear. . . . What he learns is never what he pictured, or imagined, and so he begins to be afraid. . . . Every step of learning is a new task. The fear the man is experiencing begins to mount mercilessly, unyieldingly. . . . And thus he has stumbled on the first of his natural enemies: Fear! A terrible enemy—treacherous and difficult to overcome.

People who do not have tempers, who do not feel angry or jealous, who do not get frightened—do not exist. When we turn these emotions into something constructive, we learn from them. They can add something positive to our lives. Emotional pain, like physical pain, indicates that something needs to be corrected. Used as a guide, emotional pain can expand your awareness and emotional growth. The result can be increased personal strength and greater wisdom. More important, we become united with others when we can emphathize with their pain. We come to realize that human pain which is universal and timeless unites us all.

EMOTIONAL STYLE

Most of us experience emotional cycles: up, normal, or down. Many of us, moreover, can identify ourselves as having an emotional style:

Peak Style

A "peaker" experiences feelings of movement, energy, and motivation. Such people often feel a sense of power and confidence and can cope with many things. Yet they do have low moments, periods of depression, and areas in which they feel vulnerable or less valuable.

Plateau Style

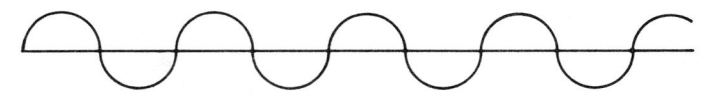

These people appear well adjusted and balanced emotionally. They may lack a bit of excitement but then they don't stay depressed. They basically feel that life is all right. Usually they are in control, plan ahead, avoid risks, rationalize, and sublimate their deepest emotions to avoid pitfalls.

Valley Style

Valley people often experience depression and emotional pain. They have deep feelings and often feel split in their depths from the ordinary daily routine. Deep feelings, although painful, make us fully aware of being alive in our pain.

No one can recommend any particular emotional style to anyone else. Each person chooses his or her emotional life "for the best of all possible reasons." There are positive and negative aspects of each of these three emotional styles; each style is very real to the person experiencing it. Many of us experience each of them at different times.

OWNING YOUR FEELINGS

One of the most difficult aspects of dealing with emotions is *owning* them. It feels as if they sweep over us, that we have no control. No one can *make* you feel anything without your cooperation. When you are willing to take personal responsibility for your emotions, you can increase your awareness of how feelings color the fabric of your life. Bertrand Russell said: "Even more important than knowledge is the life of the emotions." Without emotions, life would be flat and meaningless.

Write out a statement of responsibility for your feelings. For example:

Being anxious is inside me. When I feel anxious with someone, I owe it to myself and to him and to the relationship to share this feeling with him. I will tell him that I recognize my feeling which I am expressing, that I am aware of it as inside of me and unrelated to him. It is my own reaction and I want to share with him the distress and discomfort of my feeling. I feel that expressing the anxiety will help me get in touch with it and get off it. As I talk about it, the feeling changes. And I wait in apprehension for his responses. For I have risked telling him my feelings. And I trust him to respond as honestly and as authentically as he can.

The limits of my language are the limits of my world.
                                            Wittgenstein

7

How Language Communicates

The gift of speech is one way in which human beings can be distinguished from other animals. No tribe has ever been found without a language. We use language to create a structure of our world, and then we attempt to communicate our individual representations of that world to other people.

Every known group of human beings teaches its young the language of its culture. The learning of language is so subtle that it becomes an unconscious process. Language is a system of symbols people use to communicate with one another. Yet linguists fail to explain the mysteries of communicating because communication is more a people process than simply a language process. It is the *way* people use language that results in communication.

WATCHING YOUR LANGUAGE

In using language, we use *symbols*. Symbols have no meaning in and of themselves—only people create meaning. The symbol is not reality: the *word* "chair" is not the thing we sit in. We get into trouble when we think that words are the things themselves. *Concrete* words like chair, table, and book do not cause the same communication problems as *abstract* words like love, courage, and patriotism. *Specific* words like "my black poodle" create clearer images than *general* words like "my pet." Emotion-laden words like communism which are *connotative* affect both speaker and listener more than *denotative* words which do not carry added meaning. An awareness of the effect of words, labels, judgments—on both speaker and listener—can lead to better communication with the self and others.

HOW I USE LANGUAGE

In communicating with language, we can expect the following: inaccuracy, incompleteness, misunderstanding. These expectations can contribute to greater clarity and precision in the use of language. To use language more effectively is a lifelong goal.

- Describe a situation in which you were really pleased with what you had to say and satisfied with the results.

- Describe a situation in which you experienced difficulty, frustration, or discomfort with what you said and the results.

- List your personal strengths in communicating. For example: my vocabulary, my choice of words, my calm voice.

- List your weaknesses in communicating. For example: I get off the topic, I talk too much.

USING AND ABUSING WORDS

When you use specific, concrete words you increase the clarity and precision of your communication.

- Go through your journal and circle *abstract* words like *love, anxiety, personality,* and *communication.* Now try to make some of those words more concrete by describing, defining, giving examples, or in some way clarifying what you meant. Remind yourself to stop your thinking process (stop talking to yourself) when you find yourself indulging in hazy abstractions. Make a conscious attempt to clarify the words you choose when you are talking to yourself.

- Go through your journal and circle the *general* words. See if you can make them more specific. In place of the word *boss*, write in a name. In place of the word *work*, write in the word *the bank,* and then cross that out and write *my desk.* Use specific names to identify objects and people . . . in your thinking as well as in your writing. If your intention is to become more precise with your choice of words, it will happen for you.

- Go through your journal and circle the emotional (connotative) words. Look at your feelings and intentions with these choices. Change them to nonjudgmental or descriptive words (denotative words). Say the sentence out loud with nonemotional words. Change it back and say the sentence aloud as you wrote it. Now make a conscious choice of the word you want to use. Either or both? One word will be more of a thought, the other word more an emotion.

WORKING WITH ABSTRACT WORDS

In his book The Peter Prescription, *Laurence J. Peter made three lists of words which he calls jargon. He says that he can select at random one word from each list, sprinkle in a few words, and produce as many phrases as he needs to answer questions, make speeches, or write letters to most agencies. Choose one word from each of these lists of abstract words and see what you get.*

1	2	3
environmental	motivation	process
instructional	cognitive	concept
professional	culture	interface
perceptual	maturation	adjustment
homogeneous	creative	philosophy
sequential	relationship	articulation
developmental	accelerated	resource
exceptional	orientation	activity
socialized	guidance	curriculum
individualized	situation	approach

DANGEROUS WORDS AND RESPONSES

Go through your journal and circle any of the following words or responses that result in defensive communication. You do not need to change them; just become aware of them.

Words	*Absolutes*
either . . . or	everybody . . . nobody
but . . . no	everywhere . . . nowhere
should . . . shouldn't	everything . . . nothing
why? . . . because	always . . . never
is	all . . . none . . . only
right . . . wrong	*Responses*
good . . . bad	name calling
true . . . false	interpreting
that's a fact	reassuring
I know	probing
Labels	humoring
lazy, immature, stupid	commanding
nice, pretty, handsome, good	threatening
Generalizations	advising
nobody ever changes	preaching
nothing ever happens	instructing
nobody loves me	criticizing
	praising

INHIBITING LANGUAGE

Inhibiting words and expressions that block growth can be changed.

From	*To*
If only I had . . .	Next time I will . . .
I can't . . .	I choose not to . . .
I need . . .	I want . . .
I'm helpless . . .	I would like your help . . .
It's not my fault . . .	I am responsible . . .
You . . .	I . . .
They . . .	We . . .
It's the way I am . . .	My potential for change is . . .

LABELS AND STEREOTYPES

Although labels and stereotypes simplify our lives, they also freeze and limit our perceptions and responses.

- On a piece of paper write the following headings: then write five adjectives to describe each one.

    | Jews | Hispanics | police officers | politicians | men |
    | Asians | Germans | doctors | attorneys | women |
    | Blacks | Italians | teachers | judges | teenagers |
    | Catholics | Latins | salespeople | | |

- Notice your use of language. How often do you use labels? Make a list of labels you use about yourself. Then make a list of labels you hear others use.

- Go through your journal and circle all the "is" and "are" labels. Then rewrite your sentences without that word. For example:

    I am stupid! Sometimes I do not think before I act.

    You are insensitive! Sometimes you are not sensitive to my feelings.

- Ritual language often has little meaning. One example is apologizing. An apology is often a good way of having the last word. Saying "I'm sorry," for example, can leave the other person feeling trapped or unfulfilled.

    1. Write about a time when someone said "I'm sorry" and you felt somehow that the transaction was incomplete.

    2. Write about a time when you got out of something by using an apology.

    3. Begin a list of ritual language experiences which leave you feeling as if the transaction between you and another person is in some way unfulfilled.

JUDGMENTS

Watch for judgment words. The following exercises will help bring them to your attention.

- Go through the last three papers you wrote and identify each statement. Write *F* for fact, *A* for assumption, or *J* for judgment, and then total them. What is the ratio or balance? Do you judge more often than you make statements of fact? Rewrite the judgments to make it clear that the label is not in the object or person but in your own perceptions. For example: the statement "My son is mature" can be changed to "I feel that at times my son behaves in ways that are mature for his age." Remember that both positive labels and negative labels—both compliments and criticism—are judgments.

- Compliments are judgments. Notice compliments given to you this week. Write them down. How do they make you feel? What does each compliment tell you about the person who gave it?

LANGUAGE AND CONTEXT

By exploring how our language changes from context to context, we can gain more control over what we communicate to others.

- How does your language change when you talk to a parent or a friend? How does your mother/father's language change when they talk to you or to a friend? How do you account for such changes in language?

- Go through a passage of your writing and evaluate yourself on how precisely you use words.

- Begin to notice the precision with which you and others choose words in your conversations. Write a page of dialogue, giving each character distinctive language patterns.

THE LANGUAGE OF "RIGHT" AND "WRONG"

Quarreling means trying to show that the other person is wrong. We have some social agreements as to what is "right" and what is "wrong." Listen for these expressions:

How would you like it if I did that to you?

Give me a bite of your ice cream. I gave you a bite of mine!

I was here first.

Leave him alone. He isn't doing anything to you.

You promised.

That's not fair.

You're being selfish.

Why did you do that?

The issue of right and wrong comes from our social agreements about what is decent behavior, what is fair. Most of us have had similar moral teaching. We believe we "should" behave in certain ways. When we do not behave in these ways—and often we do not—then we make excuses for ourselves or give reasons why we do not practice the behavior we expect from others. Instead of saying "I have my own standard of right and wrong!", we say: "Well, I wasn't feeling well." "I was sick." "I forgot." "I was broke." "Well, my brother just got into town and . . ." "Oh, I didn't know you wanted that."

Moral education is usually part of the hidden curriculum in our education. There seem to be some universal laws of morality. Can you think of a country where people are admired for running away in battle or where a woman feels proud if she cheats people who have been kind to her? Also there are many moral laws specific to a particular culture such as our own. The problem is that our moral education is often an impossible "double-bind" situation. For example:

Win at any cost—Be a good loser!

Grades are not important—High grades get you into the best colleges!

Cooperation is more desirable than competition—Be successful!

To help you spot such double binds in our society, try making a list of hidden moral rules.

THE ART OF MAKING EXCUSES

When we don't behave according to unwritten but socially agreed upon rules or ethics, we often try to excuse ourselves by finding special reasons to justify our behavior.

- Make a list of the excuses you use for behaving in ways that you have been taught are wrong.

- Make a list of behavior you believe is wrong. Then make a list of behavior you've been *taught* is wrong.

- Make a list of times you have tried to make someone feel wrong.

- Make a list of times someone has tried to make you feel wrong.

- Note the excuses and justifications. Now think up some new responses. For example: "I hear you." "Thank you." "Okay."

- Note ostensible questions that are really attempts to make you wrong. For example: "Why did you do that?" Children often reply: "I don't know." As we grow older, we find "acceptable" excuses or justifications. Keep a record of these.

- Make a list of excuses our society uses for breaking moral laws. For example: Do not kill . . . except for punishment or war.

THE LIMITS OF LANGUAGE

As valuable as language is to us, it is by necessity limiting and creates an invisible prison. A word creates "a dog", "a cat", "a man." It fixes their nature, their shape, their essence. A word freezes a concept and thus sets boundaries to our thoughts. With every verbalized thought, a door shuts as we accept a world view given us by others. Unconsciously, without intention, we become wardens of the language that imprisons us.

Yet we are endowed with a wisdom that can lead us to seek keys to our self-made prisons. We exist magically within individual bodies that can create visions beyond the limits of language. Through the evolution of both individual and mass consciousness, we continually expand our boundaries day by day.

NONCOMMUNICATION THROUGH LANGUAGE

Speech habits that are thoughtless or attack the listener can be classified as noncommunication.

- Add to this list of clichés and trite expressions: "Have a nice day." "That's the name of the game." "Everybody agrees that . . ." "Let me make one thing perfectly clear."

- Add to this list of "cutoffs" (thoughtless words, expressions): "Don't worry . . ." "Don't feel that way . . ."

- Write about a time when someone cut you off by switching the topic.

- Give an example of a time when you cut someone off.

HOW WELL DO YOU LISTEN?

We can learn to listen better if we acknowledge that listening, unlike breathing, is not a natural process. It can be improved by intention *and by* practice.

- Listening often depends on the situation. Choose a particular situation and write about the blocks to listening you experienced. For example: a lecture, a sales pitch, a friend who was trying to persuade you against your will.

- In what situations do you have difficulty listening?

- Write about ways in which you "tune out" people. Do you have a pattern of *not* listening? Do you have different patterns with different people?

- In what situations do you listen best? What are your patterns of attentive listening? Do you ask questions? Take notes? Watch gestures?

ACKNOWLEDGMENTS

If you acknowledge communication even though you don't comprehend, then it's unreal for both sender and receiver.

- Write about a time when you only pretended to understand another person.

- Write about a time when you think another person only pretended to understand you.

- Make a list of words or expressions you can use to *acknowledge* others. For example: "I got it." "Good." "Fine." "Yes." "Thank you." "I understand."

MEANINGS OF SILENCE

Edgar Lee Masters in his poem "Silence" inquiries:

And I ask: For the depths
Of what use is language?

When we are with another, sharing the stars and the moon, music or death, we often find ourselves speechless. Artists and musicians sometimes can capture love, hatred, sorrow, and hope without words. In fact, silence can be a form of communicating our deepest emotions.

- Are you uncomfortable with silence?

- What do you do with silence?

- How do you interpret the silence of another person?

- Write several examples of how you used silence in communicating. Describe how you felt and what you did.

- Make two lists that express the possible meanings of silence. For example:

anger	contentment
pain	communion
discontent	interest
disapproval	peace of mind
boredom	a quietness of spirit
insecurity	sharing with another
confusion	caring/listening
fear/anxiety	love
depression	understanding
withdrawal	happiness
sadness	support
hopelessness	approval
avoidance	involvement

Man's mind stretched to a new idea never goes back to its original dimensions.
     Oliver Wendell Holmes

8

How the Mind Communicates

The human brain is the most delicate and complex mechanism in all creation. In fact, we have learned so little about how the brain works that we cannot even call the study of the mind a science. We speculate about how it operates. We have, however, found some ways of thinking that affect communicating—such as abstracting, stereotyping, and classifying facts, assumptions, and judgments. Some of the most exciting studies of the way the mind works deal with meditation, imagery, dreams, biofeedback research, and hypnosis.

Experiments indicate that our minds have far greater potential than we have experienced. The meditation, dream, imagination, and fantasy exercises presented in the following pages provide us with new alternative ways of thinking. Moreover, writing your experiences will illustrate to you how your mind communicates.

In this chapter, we will explore different ways we think. We will look at the ways we generalize and stereotype. We will talk about justifying or rationalizing what we say or do. And we will explore the effects of beliefs, expectations, and disappointments on ourselves and others.

DIFFERENT WAYS WE THINK

Some of us are better in mathematics than in language. Others are better in art than in music. This activity is designed to explore the different ways we think.

- Describe your ability to put your thoughts into language.

- We can think with mathematical symbols. Describe your mathematical ability.

- *Analysis* is the process of taking things apart. Discuss your ability to analyze ideas, books, and works of art. *Synthesis* is the process of putting things together. When you write a research paper, you synthesize many different sources of information into a unified whole. How well do you synthesize information?

- Have you ever studied logic? Describe your ability to think logically.

- Objective thinking is appropriate in some situations. At other times, subjective responses seem more appropriate. How flexible are you in fitting objective or subjective thinking to different situations? Write examples of each.

- Our culture stresses some modes of thinking at the expense of others—for example, analytical thinking is rewarded in college with high grades, units, and degrees. How successful have you been in developing your own preferred modes of thinking? What can you do to strengthen your weaknesses in thinking?

- Different mind processes may conflict inside a single individual. Write about your experiences of conflict with different ways of thinking.

OVERGENERALIZING AND STEREOTYPING

Becoming aware of overgeneralizations and stereotypes can help us communicate more precisely and effectively.

- Notice whenever you or another person use the words *all, every, none,* and *no one.*
- Write down overgeneralizations you hear or use. For example: Students always . . . Parents . . . Blacks . . . Teachers . . . Women . . . Men . . .
- Ask others to listen for your generalizations and add their observations to your list.
- Write a paper telling yourself what stereotyping does for you. What do you gain? What do you lose?

BELIEFS

A belief is a confidence in an alleged fact without any proof. We all have beliefs about life, death, God, and people. These beliefs become unstated and unconscious parts of our symbolic worlds. They affect our perceptions, feelings, and behavior. Explore and clarify for yourself some of your beliefs:

- Write a list of things you believe in: I believe . . .

- Write a list of things you don't believe in: I don't believe in . . .

- Write about a disagreement you have had with someone whose beliefs differ from yours.

- Write about your feelings when someone disagrees with your beliefs.

- What do you do when someone disagrees with your beliefs?

- Write about your feelings when another person agrees with your beliefs.

- Do you choose friends who agree with you most of the time?

CLOSED MIND VS. OPEN MIND

When an individual has a closed cognitive organization of beliefs and disbeliefs about reality, he or she is not open to beliefs that are different. Open-minded people evaluate messages more objectively and differentiate between shades of meaning. They are more provisional and more willing to modify beliefs. This exercise will help you find out where you fit on the continuum between open- and closed-mindedness.

- Think of a topic to which you react in the following ways: rigid, stubborn, unwilling to compromise.

- Think of a person and a situation to which you react in the following ways: rigid, stubborn, unwilling to compromise.

- Think of a person and a situation to which another person reacted to you in the following ways: rigid, stubborn, unwilling to compromise.

- Think of a subject to which you responded in the following ways: flexible, broad-minded, willing to listen.

- Recall a time when you responded to a person in the following ways: flexible, broad-minded, willing to listen.

JUSTIFYING AND RATIONALIZING

Finding explanations for why things work the way they do can be a fascinating mental exercise and can result in great new discoveries. But giving reasons about *why* you act the way you do or why you feel the way you do usually results in justifications or rationalizations. Reasons are seldom of use in relationships or in human communication. If you are aware of the words *why* and *because* in your communication with others, you can choose to continue to relate that way. But if you are not conscious of their effects, you may not be choosing.

In a world without certainty, we often *work* at making others wrong. When we relate through a "right/wrong" orientation, we try to make ourselves right by giving reasons. Justifying and rationalizing are ways to excuse ourselves or make ourselves right. We live in a culture that expects reasons, explanations, justifications. Become conscious of them; *experience* how they feel. Then decide whether you want to continue explaining and giving reasons for yourself.

- Become aware of your uses of the words "why" and "because."
- Go through your writing and circle every *why* and every *because*.
- See if you can substitute expressions like: *when, how, what, where,* and *who: When* did that happen? *How* did that happen? *What* happened? *Where* did that happen? *Who* was there when that happened?

EXPECTATIONS

An expectation is a confidence that a certain event will happen. When we expect too much of ourselves or others, we often experience disappointment. This activity is designed to help you explore your expectations and their effects on yourself and your relationships.

- Pick different people and write about your expectations of them.

- How do you feel when they do not fulfill your expectations?

- What do you do?

- Write your specific expectation of the people you live with. For example: "I expect my son to . . ."

- Explain how this person does or does not live up to your expectations.

- How do you react when your expectations are not met?

HANDLING DISAPPOINTMENT

Becoming aware of how we handle disappointment can help motivate us to change unrealistic expectations.

- When your expectations result in disappointment, how do you handle your feelings? Do you:
    1. Complain, blame, become belligerent? (Do you think: "If I complain, people will do what I want," "If I stick up for my rights, I'll get my way" or "The squeaky wheel gets the grease"?)
    2. Please others, accept authority, change yourself? (Do you think: "If I don't fight, they'll see how nice I am and do what I want" or "If I do what they say, they'll leave me alone"?)
    3. Pretend, put up a front, try to impress? (Do you think: "If they see I don't care or that I'm important, they'll do what I want"?)

CONTEMPLATION

Contemplation is a mental activity. To contemplate is to view with attention, to observe thoughtfully, or to reflect upon. Action ranks so high in the value system of our culture that contemplation is not appreciated. Even the aged and retired rarely wish to lead a life of contemplation. We have not been taught to contemplate. Contemplation is not simply thinking about something or reminiscing. It is a special type of mental activity hardly known in our culture. Here are three questions to provoke your thinking on the subject:

1. What do you suppose is involved in the mental activity of contemplation?
2. Can you name some men and women who know how to contemplate? What evidence is there of such mental activity? What kind of a process is it?
3. What is wisdom? Do you know anyone you think is wise? What types of men and women do we designate as having wisdom?

MIND POTENTIAL

Recent experiments with biofeedback prove that the mind influences the biochemical and physiological functions of the body. Machines have been built that measure our ability to change our brain waves, heart rate, blood pressure, oxygen level, skin temperature, galvanic skin response, and muscle tension. I once experienced having an electrode attached to my left middle finger. A wire was connected to a temperature machine which recorded my skin temperature and gave me two kinds of feedback: visual (degrees on a meter) and auditory (a click-click-click noise as my skin temperature increased).

I took a few minutes to relax completely. I then *visualized* holding my hands up to a hot fire in my fireplace at home. I could hear the machine going click-click-click. The experimenter who was watching the machine while I had my eyes closed said, "You have increased your temperature two degrees in two minutes." I then decided to switch the image. I imagined that I was holding a large block of ice in my left hand. My hand hurt so much that I had to switch the image to holding a glass with ice and water in it. I could not hear any sounds from the machine. The experimenter said, "You have dropped your temperature four degrees in two minutes."

I had never had any training on a biofeedback machine. But I do practice visualization and imagery. And I have trained myself in deep relaxation. I share this episode with you because I know about biofeedback machines from experience rather than from reading about them as you are doing now. Knowing through *experience* is very different from knowing through reading.

Mind control has long been practiced, both in Eastern religions and in the West. A form of self-hypnosis was practiced by monks in the Middle Ages. Current research indicates interconnections between mind, emotions, and body. Lie detector tests use a number of different machines that measure body and emotional responses, although we cannot be sure they can tell if a person is lying or not. The machines used in biofeedback research these days are very crude compared to what will be developed in the future. We are only at the foot of the mountain in the exploration of the human mind's potential.

THE SPLIT MIND

Freud claimed that the mind is divided into the conscious, the preconscious (latent but capable of being tapped), and the unconscious (repressed). He explained behavior in terms of id, ego, and superego. Eric Berne talked about The Parent, The Adult, and The Child voices. Socrates compared the human soul to a chariot drawn by two horses—one black, one white—pulling in different directions and weakly controlled by a charioteer.

Modern brain research is beginning to explore the bases for all the different theories of the mind that have been developed over the centuries. Robert Ornstein, in *The Psychology of Consciousness,* writes about the left and right hemispheres of the brain. Dividing the wrinkled outer structure of the brain in half, from front to back, is a tissue of fibers by which information can be transmitted from one hemisphere to the other. Ornstein says that each hemisphere shares the potential for many functions. Most activities require the use of both hemispheres, he claims, yet most of us tend to specialize, using the left or the right parts of the cerebrum.

The *left* hemisphere controls the right side of the body and specializes in abstraction, logic, time, sequential information, verbalization, analysis, and mathematics. The *right* hemisphere controls the left side of the body and specializes in space, aesthetics, art, music, spirituality, body image, recognition of faces, intuition, fantasy, and visualization. Most of our formal education stresses reading, writing, and arithmetic—left-brain functions. Today educators are exploring ways to teach those abilities less developed such as imagery and visualization.

EXPLORING THE SPLIT BRAIN

Most people tend to emphasize either left brain or right-brain functions. Developing the less-used functions can help us live richer lives. Have someone read the following directions to you (or put them on a tape and play them on a tape recorder).

1. Sit with your eyes closed and relax.

2. Now get in touch with your breathing. Just notice how your breath comes in and out of your body.

3. Now start at the top of your head and slowly begin to relax muscles: first the top of your head, forehead, around your eyes and mouth, neck, shoulders and arms, chest and back, waist, stomach, thighs, calves, feet, toes. Are your hands relaxed?

4. Now imagine yourself floating upward out of your chair. See yourself float out the room, above the building, the city, the state, the country, the world. See yourself out in space looking back at the earth. See and feel yourself moving toward Mars.

5. Now imagine yourself to be a Martian. Notice your shape and size. See yourself moving and notice how your muscles feel as you move. Listen. Do you hear any sounds? Are there any odors? Do you feel warm or cold? What do you see around you?

6. Now write about your experience.

While you are using your imagination, you are using the right-brain functions. When you write down your experience, you are using the left-brain functions. Actually, we use both sides simultaneously; yet one side or the other carries more activity at any particular time, depending upon whether we are visualizing or verbalizing.

MEDITATION

In essence, meditation is the process of emptying the mind, withdrawing from the physical world, and turning inward toward the real self. In this place, a person can find peace, quiet, images, voices, visions. Most of us have devoted much of our lives to conscious thought: to controlling our outer world. Meditation is a state of letting go. For many of us, letting go of the controls is a frightening act. Yet an attitude of quiet can become a pleasure if you allow yourself to flow in unstructured time, experiencing a serene harmony.

Meditation, like swimming, cannot be experienced until you jump in. You cannot jump in, however, without some suggestions about how to float. Real water can be a hazard for the nonswimmer, but meditation presents no physical threat. It can create anxiety, though, if you have expectations, if you judge your performance, if you set yourself up for disappointment. Here are some suggestions:

1. Choose a quiet time and place when you are not tired. Dim lighting helps. Allow yourself ten to fifteen minutes.

2. Sit in a comfortable chair, back erect, feet flat on the floor, hands folded in your lap.

3. Say to yourself: "I am now withdrawing from the everyday world." Empty your mind of thoughts. If a thought comes to you, say: "Let it go for now."

4. Allow all your muscles to relax, from the top of your head, down your body, to your toes.

5. Create something (a sound, a word, a melody) as a focus of attention—a rhythmical sound like *Da* . . . da . . . da . . . da . . . (emphasis on the first syllable)—and repeat the sound over and over in your mind. Or concentrate on your breathing (in . . . out, in . . . out).

6. If your mind goes back to thoughts, to problems, to analyzing, simply say: "Now come back and relax, and let go." Begin the rhythmical sound again or concentrate on the breathing.

7. If you find yourself criticizing or judging what you are doing, simply say to yourself: "That's okay. Now relax again, let go again."

8. As you practice, you will find you can empty your mind for longer periods of time. If you hear sounds, that's all right. If thoughts flicker across your mind, let it happen. Then get back to the flow: let go again.

9. After you practice for several days, you will notice an increase in sensitivity and energy after meditating. You may wish to join a meditation group or read a book on meditation. There are as many ways to meditate as there are people. Find whatever works best for you to enrich your creativity and physical well-being.

RECORDING YOUR DREAMS

A dream does not need to be dissected or analyzed. We do not have a "science" of dreams that tells us how to figure them out or interpret their meaning. Dreams can provide entertainment, of course, like any good drama. But there is also a serious side to dreams: scientists tell us that dreams keep us sane by repairing the damage done each day in the process of living. Here are some theories about dreams:

1. They may enact solutions to unresolved problems.
2. They may be a way of expressing feelings we are unaware of.
3. They may compensate for what is missing in our lives.
4. They may show us the other side of things and increase our awareness of what is around and within us.
5. They may be a way of looking at our fears, prejudices, and pretenses.
6. They may be a place to acknowledge parts of ourselves.
7. They may be a source of creativity, a source of discovery, a release of intuition and insight.
8. They may contribute to scientific discovery and artistic creativity.

Whatever dreams may do, probably no single interpretation will fit more than one person or one dream, so generalizations are unimportant. If you do not ordinarily remember your dreams, here are some suggestions. Keep a notebook and pencil by your bed. Write in it the moment you come to consciousness. (Dreams fade in the first few minutes.) First tell the dream, relive the experience, include the feelings, and give an overall impression. Then feel your way back through it, listen to it, imagine it, allow it simply to be a dream without diagnosing it.

TYPES OF IMAGINATION

Every image tends to produce the physical conditions and the external acts corresponding to it. Often psychologists or advertisers refer to this power of imagination as *suggestion*. Every movement requires a previous image of the movement to be executed—which makes visualization a necessary stage for action. There is, nevertheless, a distinction between conscious visualization of an image deliberately chosen and the imaginative function which is spontaneous and operates on unconscious levels. *Reproductive* imagination can be deliberately evoked. *Creative* imagination is spontaneous and occurs when it occurs. It cannot be willed.

Reproductive Imagination

Reproductive imagination can be an image or set of images of what we have already seen or experienced. We can also consciously evoke images of something we have never seen by combining elements previously experienced. If you have seen movies about death and rebirth, you can reproduce images of those experiences. You can imagine heaven or hell. Reproductive imagination can be improved through exercise. Its practice also improves other functions such as concentration, will power, observation, and memorization. Visualization and imagery have many *practical* uses. Although we cannot discuss all of them here, the following are examples of a few. Imagery can be as unique and original as you wish it to be. Here are some of its practical uses:

1. Increased self-awareness and insight
2. Personality change, character development, attitude change
3. Relieving stress, receiving additional energy, improving health
4. Behavior modification, desensitization, reduction of blocks and habits
5. Problem-solving, reaching goals, finding purpose in life
6. Sensitivity to others, increased ability to love and understand others, enriched personal relationships
7. Development in the arts: painting, music, writing
8. Creativity, intuition, discovery, new perceptions
9. Sports, dancing, athletics, body coordination
10. Developing study habits, concentration, academic skills

Before we go on to specific examples and techniques, you should recognize that if you want change you must choose only one or two very specific changes and work on them. It may take fifteen minutes twice a day for fifteen or twenty days before you note a cumulative effect. Research indicates that a large proportion of people who actually participate in reproductive imagination workshops can improve the right-brain functions. After the workshop, some people find they can practice while doing mundane chores or even while driving. For those who often carry on a dialogue with themselves (a left-brain function), images can begin to take form as they practice visualization. This kind of symmetry and balance is the goal. Many great scientists and artists write about their creative insights as occurring in visions or images first. Einstein *experienced* most of his basic principles of the relativity of distance, time, and mass through imagery and visualization before he attempted to verbalize them.

Creative Imagination

Creative imagination is spontaneous. It may come like dreams in the night when you are relaxed and your mind is empty. There is a stage between waking and sleeping called the *hypnogogic state*—many creative people claim that stories, visions, solutions to scientific research, and other great creative images have come to them at this time. Some people have developed the ability to prolong this state. One method is to lie in bed with your forearm up and the hand extended toward the ceiling. When your arm drops, this brings you back before you fall asleep. People who have learned to prolong creative mind states develop the images into art projects, writing, music, and scientific discoveries. One productive method is called *guided imagery*.

Guided Imagery

If guided imagery sounds intriguing, you can ask a friend to lead you. Including relaxation time, a guided imagery usually takes about fifteen minutes. In any event, just reading about the process can start you experiencing imagination in a new way. Whenever you close your eyes and relax, if you can quiet your mind and empty it of words, you can learn to alter your level of consciousness. In biofeedback training, for example, people learn to recognize changing brainwaves. You too can become aware of a changing state in brain functioning without machines if you experience it. Close your eyes and empty your mind. Be fully relaxed. Whenever you notice that your mind is thinking words, simply go back to visualizing a white room with white walls, ceiling, and floor. Or imagine you are looking at a white movie screen and whatever appears on that screen is all right. Pay attention to feelings inside your head. Notice any brief, delicate sensations that are more pleasant than the rest. Imagine yourself in a meadow. Breathe deeply and feel the oxygen coursing through your body. Keep breathing effortlessly and pleasantly. Lie down in the meadow and look up at the sky. Simply look at the sky and notice any sensations inside your head . . . relaxing is letting go. You cannot will yourself to let go. Whenever you find yourself trying, let that go too. "Trying" is willpower, which will prevent you from getting onto another level of consciousness.

Visualization involves creating images in your mind: shapes with color; sounds or sights; odors or tastes. Most of us, if we close our eyes, can reexperience in our imaginations the world of our sensations. There are techniques to make visualizations easier—a serene setting, an ability to relax the body and mind, an intention to let go. Attitude is important. You cannot direct your mind. A willingness to be without intent or design creates better images. You must be willing to let go of judging, analyzing, and expectations. The value of visualization is in the experiencing.

Imageries can be free-floating inner processes or they can be guided in the sense that someone gives you directions about a trip into your inner space. You can create any number of guided imageries for others and they can create any number for you.

You can do them alone, with another person, or with a tape recorder or cassette. First get into a deeply relaxed state. Your mind feels clear, tranquil, directionless: without plan or will. It is open and receptive to images that will be helpful to you. Whatever comes into your mind is all right. If nothing comes, that is all right too. Simply experience whatever happens.

Guided Imagery I

Sit with your back straight and your feet on the floor. Relax and close your eyes. Get in touch with your breathing. Take three or four deep breaths. Now visualize yourself standing in a fog. See a black wall begin to appear in the fog in front of you. In the wall, see a door with a gold doorknob. In the center of the door, see a white plaque. Write a word, image, or symbol on the white plaque. When you are ready, go inside the door. Observe all that is before you. What do you see? Can you hear any sounds? Can you smell anything? Feel the temperature in the room. Be aware of a presence beside you. Ask the presence the meaning of this scene. Let any appropriate conversation take place with the presence. Now the scene changes. Observe what the new scene is like. Ask the presence to explain the new scene and its meaning to you. Get ready to leave. Walk to the door. When you are ready to walk out of the room, walk through the door. Stop and look back at the door. Is the word or symbol the same or different? Walk out into the fog. Now open your eyes and write down your experience.

Guided Imagery II

You are fully relaxed, deeply relaxed. Notice your breathing. Your eyes are closed; your mind is receptive. Imagine yourself walking through a meadow. There is a stream . . . see it and hear it. Feel the sun on your skin. See yourself. (How are you dressed? How do you walk and feel?) Walk across the meadow to a grove of trees. Walk into the shade of the trees and feel the difference. At the end of the grove, through to the other side, see a chapel. Walk into the chapel. In the chapel is a painting . . . look at all the details and colors. Down the hall is a statue . . . note its design, texture, shape, size. There is music . . . listen to it. There are three doors. You will now have one minute to go through each door into each room. Choose one door: open it and walk in. What is on the other side? Notice all the details, the sounds, the temperature. When you are ready, go back out into the hall and enter the second room and experience what is there. And when you are ready, go into the third room. When you are through exploring, walk out of the chapel, back into the meadow. When you are ready, open your eyes and write about your experience.

Guided Imagery III

You are fully relaxed, deeply relaxed. Notice your breathing. Your eyes are closed; your mind is receptive. Imagine yourself leaving this room. Walk out into the street and decide on a direction. Go in that direction . . . wherever it takes you . . . across the city, over the hills, through fields and meadows . . . notice whatever you see:

observe the details (the grass and flowers). Stop and experience. Visualize a mountain in the distance. Slowly climb the mountain. Scale the heights until you reach the peak. What do you see? A wise man comes to you and sits quietly by your side. You can ask him any question you want. (Listen to his answer.) You can carry on any conversation you wish or you can sit quietly. When you are ready, come back.

Guided Imagery IV

You are fully relaxed. Notice your breathing. Your eyes are closed. Imagine your birth . . . go back and visualize and reexperience your birth. Watch yourself again as a baby and see how you change as you grow. Slowly go stage by stage through your childhood, recalling and remembering whatever comes up for you: home, school, friends. Whatever comes, reexperience those times. Reexperience your life, phase by phase, stage by stage, until you catch up with your life today. Now imagine where you will be and what you will look like ten years from now. Now imagine where you will be and what you will look like when you are seventy or eighty years old. Who are you with? What kind of transportation do you have? How do you move around? What are you wearing? Where are you living? Now imagine your death . . . visualize and experience what it is like to die. Imagine yourself in a beautiful, peaceful place without a body, without a physical entity. What is that place like? What do you feel like? Now a voice tells you: "Tomorrow is a special day. One day in every ten thousand years everyone who is dead can choose to go back to earth. But you cannot choose in what form you will go back. You will go back to earth in some other form than your present self. Do you want to go back?" If you decide to go back, look and see what you are. What form have you taken? What are you?

NEW DIRECTIONS

New research on "hemisphere thinking" indicates that the right hemisphere operates by evoking totalities. A whiff of perfume may conjure up an early love affair; a photo may recreate an entire past experience; a melody may recall a previous relationship. The "language" of the right hemisphere seems to be metaphoric as well as sensory and holistic. Thus aphorisms, poetry, and Zen koans allow us to see ourselves and our behavior in a totally new light. When we can perceive our world in new ways, we expand our horizons and create new modes for operating in the world. When the left hemisphere gets overloaded or confused with contradiction, ambiguity, or paradox, we might well move into the nonverbal hemisphere with imagery, sounds, and figurative language where we can create new images of ourselves and others.

Well-done is better than well-said.
Benjamin Franklin

9

How Actions Communicate

We communicate information about ourselves through what we do. Actions are observable by others and they communicate messages. Our culture teaches us how to behave. We develop habitual patterns of behavior that are often difficult to change. And because our behavior is not always consistent, we feel confused at times.

In this chapter we will explore the roles we have learned to act out, and some of the automatic responses we make in our daily living. Then we can write about ways to change our own behavior: behavior modification, guided imagery, autosuggestion, and setting goals.

Sometimes behavior, our own or that of another person, is a problem to us. We run into trouble when we say one thing and do another. We can accept these inconsistencies, we can observe them, or we can change them. Our actions communicate something of who we are. Goethe said: "Self-knowledge is best learned, not by contemplation, but *action*. Strive to do your duty, and you will soon discover of what stuff you are made."

INTERPERSONAL NEEDS

In our relationships, we respond to people in certain ways. We need people and we want them to respond to us in certain ways. Psychologist Bill Schutz says that every individual has three interpersonal needs: *inclusion, control,* and *affection.*

Inclusion is the need to establish and maintain satisfactory relations, to be comfortable with them, to be "included." Mutual interest means being interested in others and having them be interested in you. The need to be included satisfies an individual's sense of self-esteem. *Control* is that element in a relationship which deals with power: the degree of control you have over others and how much control they have over you. A feeling of mutual respect for each other depends on how people balance a sense of competence and responsibility for themselves and others. We need to respect others and to have others respect us for our competence and responsibility. *Affection* is the need to establish and maintain love and warmth in a relationship. Mutual affection involves the ability to love other people and have them love you. When you are loved, your self-image is that you are lovable.

INCLUSION, CONTROL, AFFECTION

This activity will help you explore your needs and need satisfaction.

- On a separate sheet of paper, describe the extent to which you want to be included in groups of people: the family, at work, socially. Does the degree to which you want to be included match your experience of being included? For some people, being included in groups is far less important than other needs. They prefer to spend more time with one or two people. Is your need for inclusion satisfied by the amount you get?

- Describe the degree of control you want. Does it match what you have? Do you like to have others make decisions or do you prefer to make the decisions?

- Describe yourself in terms of your affection needs. Do you get as much affection as you want?

- Evaluate yourself on the following scales (10 is high):

	Inclusion	
Social, belonging, groups	10 ——————————————— 1	Detached, withdrawn, a loner

	Control	
Power, responsibility, decision-making	10 ——————————————— 1	Compliance, submission, dependence

	Affection	
Love, intimacy, warmth	10 ——————————————— 1	Cool, distant, uninvolved

There is no ideal place to be on these scales. The real issue is do you get what you need? Do you give what you want? Is there a discrepancy between what you say, what you do, and what you feel?

Karen Horney has developed a list of ten needs which she calls "neurotic" because they are irrational solutions to basic problems. For example, a destructive experience could predispose a person to adopt certain needs to satisfy a past problem. Even though that problem was in the past, the person may hang on to the need. All the following needs, says Horney, may be overstressed:

1. Need for affection and approval: the indiscriminate need to please others

2. Need for a partner to take over one's life: a dread of being deserted and a tendency to overvalue love as the solution to all problems

3. Need to restrict one's life: such an individual saves money, fears making demands on others, remains inconspicuous in order to avoid being hurt or disappointed

4. Need for power: a craving for authority for its own sake; disrespect for feelings or individuality of others; the need for control; contempt for "stupidity" and bad judgment; the belief in sheer willpower

5. Need to exploit others: valuing others if they have power, position, authority, or can do something for the neurotic individual

6. Need for prestige: measuring personal value by public recognition

7. Need for personal admiration: need to be admired for an "image of worth"; fear of people seeing one as one is

8. Need for personal achievement: relentless driving to higher and higher levels of achievement; need to be the best; fear of failure
9. Need for self-sufficiency and independence: keeping distance to avoid being hurt
10. Need for perfection: deep fear of making mistakes or being criticized; trying to make oneself impregnable and infallible; constantly searching for flaws in oneself

Some needs are totally self-defeating. The need for power, for example, can become insatiable. The need for independence can never be fully satisfied because another part of the person cries out to be loved and accepted. The search for perfection is a lost cause from the beginning. In their extreme forms, all these needs are unrealistic and self-defeating. Each of us has them to some degree, but most of us tend toward a sense of balance.

UNREALISTIC NEEDS

Exploring unrealistic needs can help us become more realistic in our relationships.

- In Horney's list of "neurotic" needs, which ones do you feel you have to some degree? Can you connect these needs with some past experiences?

- Make a list of ten items: To survive, I need . . . to be happy, I need . . . , and so on.

- Go back over your list of needs and see how many times you can change "I need" to "I want."

ROLES WE PLAY

In an article called "Pressures in the Classroom," the authors explored teacher roles and student roles. Depending on their style, their students, and the situation in a particular class at a particular time, teachers may find themselves playing six different roles, each appropriate in certain conditions but not necessarily compatible with the others. They may act as:

An *expert* concerned mainly with the transmission of facts and information

A formal *authority* concerned with the role of controller and agent for the college system

A *facilitator* responding to each student's definitions of his or her own goals

A *socializing agent*—guide and gatekeeper for an inner circle of specialists (anthropologists, sociologists, psychologists)

An *ego ideal*—a model of competence, enthusiasm, and energy

A *person* trying to communicate that, in addition to the role of teacher, he or she has personal interests and wants to form relationships with students in the class

Some teachers may settle for one or two of these roles; others may play different parts at different times. But every teacher's role will change as a result of his or her interaction with the students in a particular class.

In the same article in *Psychology Today,* the writers identified different student roles. These roles, they say, exert different pressures on the teacher. An analysis of the classroom behavior of fifty-nine men and forty-eight women resulted in the following eight "clusters:"

Compliant student: conventional, contented, trusting of authority, willing to go along with the teacher; usually younger than the average student

Anxious-dependent student: concerned about what the teacher thinks of him or her; low self-esteem, doubtful about competence; anxious about exams and grades

Discouraged worker: intelligent, hardworking, intellectually involved but chronically depressed and personally distant

Independent student: self-confident, interested, involved; tends to identify with teacher and see him or her as a colleague; usually older than the average student

Hero: intelligent, creative, involved; resentful of authority, rebellious, introspective; ambivalent toward teacher, erratic in performance

Sniper: defensive, low creativity, low self-esteem, uninvolved, indifferent toward class, attracted to authoritarian class structure, tendency to lash out and quickly withdraw

Attention-seeker: sociable, wants to be liked, to please, to get good grades; women flirt, men show off and joke (with men teachers); dependent on reinforcement from others

Silent student: speaks only when sure of approval; feels helpless, vulnerable, threatened in relation to teacher but longs for affection

What works for one teacher, student, or class may not work well for another. We all need to develop our abilities to recognize the emotional realities of the roles we and others play. When we become aware of the interactions, some creative responses can be experienced. Interpersonal communication happens between persons, not characters in a play. If we keep individual uniqueness in our consciousness, we will not respond to masks or stereotypes. We will look under the surface of the person and the situation.

Each individual has unique expectations, needs, and values. No teacher can hope to fulfill the expectations or needs of all the students. No parent will act the same way to all the children. No employer can hope to relate in the same way with all the employees. The individual who fears being phony, fickle, or changeable, who prizes the image of the strong-willed character who remains steadfast and constant, is simply playing another role. In addition to all the mixtures of personalities and changes in interpersonal situations, people change with time. Through awareness of the complex interactions of roles, we can learn to improve our communicating and relating.

IDENTIFYING ROLES

Since all of us act out certain roles we can benefit by taking the time to explore how these roles affect us.

- Take any interpersonal situation (parent/child; employer/employee; husband/wife; friend/friend). Write a description of your roles at one point in time. Write a description at a later time. Have your perceptions of that relationship changed? Has your behavior changed? Has the other person's behavior changed?

- Notice the difference in roles in a particular situation. For example: If you witness an auto accident, notice what the drivers do, what the police officer does, and what the witnesses do in their roles in that situation. Or notice in a hospital the defined roles of doctor, nurse, orderly, and patient. Notice your own participation and definition in a number of different situations.

- Write a page on "The Roles I Play" or "My Variety of Selves."

- Identify a word in the following list that applies to a role you play with a particular person. Or identify the roles another person plays with you. Identifying roles can help us vary and expand our ways of relating to others.

    | initiator | dominator | joker |
    | questioner | avoider | preacher/moralizer |
    | information-giver | critic | threatener |

supporter/encourager	advice-giver	commander/boss
follower	observer	analyzer
recognition-seeker	judge	sympathizer

- Write a paragraph defining the term you chose and give two or three specific examples of what you or that other person said or did that fits the role.

- Sensitize yourself to labeling. Remember that the use of a word freezes you or another person temporarily and that this label is *not* the person. Using labels can result in a self-fulfilling prophecy.

SEX ROLES

In recent years, many people have attempted to come to terms with new norms, roles, and identities. Perhaps no dimension of our experience involves us more than our sexual roles.

- On a separate sheet of paper, write about your personal feelings and experiences of yourself as a sexual being.

- Close your eyes and relax. Now imagine that your sex is reversed. If you are a male, imagine you are a female, and vice versa. How is your body different? How do you feel? How do you move and walk in your imagination? What will you do in this new body that you don't do now? Compare the experience of being this other sex with your own real sex.

- On a separate sheet of paper, write how you feel about being a man or woman.

- How do you relate to individuals of the opposite sex? The same sex?

Parent Roles

Each of us was born into a family and lived in a family. Our feelings, thoughts, and values were influenced not only by family relationships but also by the cultural values. Certain *self-perpetuating* responses, taught by one generation to the next, occur in all social groups. Become aware of them. You need not feel guilty. Simply experience the kinds of responses you make. Here are a few stock parent roles that we use in many different relationships:

The Helper: provides answers, solutions, and recommendations—"Why don't you . . . ? If I were you. . . ."

The Praiser: provides positive evaluation which is a judgment—"Good job. . . . Good person. . . . I approve. . . . That's nice."

The Supporter: reassures and sympathizes—"Don't feel bad. . . . Don't worry. . . . It'll be better tomorrow."

The Psychologist: diagnoses, analyzes, interprets—"What you need is. . . . What's wrong with you is. . . . Your problem is. . . ."

The Examiner: questions, probes, interrogates—"Why? Who? Where? What? When? How?"

The Kidder: uses sarcasm, wit, or ridicule—"Burn the school down. . . . Get up on the wrong side of the bed?"

The Diverter: avoids problems, shifts to another subject—"Let's not talk about that now. . . . Forget it. . . . Later."

The Commander: orders and directs—"You must. . . . You have to. . . . You'll do as I say."

The Threatener: warns and admonishes—"You'd better do what I say. . . . If you don't, then. . . ."

The Preacher: moralizes and obligates others—"It's your duty. . . . You ought to. . . . You should."

The Lecturer: argues and instructs—"These are the facts. . . . This is the way. . . . The truth."

The Judge: evaluates, disapproves, blames, criticizes—"You are lazy. . . . Your hair is terrible. . . . That's stupid."

EXPLORING YOUR PARENT VOICE

Write responses to the following comments as if they were made by your child (real or imagined).

- "I'm bored. I wish I had something to do. There's nothing to do around this house."

    Response:

- "I'm not going to clean my room now. I'll do it later. Stop bugging me about it!"

    Response:

- "I don't want to eat. I'm not hungry. Leave me alone!"

    Response:

- "What's the matter with me? All the other kids have a friend. Why doesn't anyone like me?"

    Response:

- "All the other kids wear their hair this way and their parents don't bug them about it. Why are you always picking on me?"

    Response:

- "I hate housework! Why do they give me so much? I'll never get it done."

    Response:

- "I'm sick and tired of getting bossed around. 'Do this . . . do that!' I'll sure be glad when I get out of this house!"

    Response:

- "All the other kids get to stay out Friday night. How come you keep treating me like a baby? When are you going to let me grow up?"

    Response:

- "I'm sick and tired of your harping on grades. I'm doing my best! Why don't you shut up?"

    Response:

- "I can't find a job and you're so tight. The other kids have parents who give them money. How come you never give me any?"

    Response:

Now go back and label your responses—The Helper, The Commander, The Preacher, and so forth.

EXPLORING YOUR CHILD VOICE

Write responses to the following as if they were given to you by your parent.

- "If you don't clean your room right now, you can't go out!"

    Response:

- "It is your responsibility to put gas in the car when you use it. You didn't do that, so you are not a responsible person."

    Response:

- "You know right from wrong. Why did you do that?"
  Response:

- "If I were you, I'd try to talk to the teacher. Go see her after school and tell her what happened."
  Response:

- "Why are you so lazy? You never do anything."
  Response:

- "As long as you live in this house, you'll do what I say!"
  Response:

- "You're a very pretty (handsome) girl (boy)."
  Response:

- "Did the teacher give you an A? That's a very good drawing."
  Response:

- "That teacher sounds like a clown. Just forget about him!"

  Response:

- "Where did you go? Who went with you? What time did you get in?"

  Response:

Now classify your responses and feelings. You may want to add to these lists:

Responses	*Feelings*
rebellious	guilt
passive	resentment
defiant	anger
hostile	fear
resistant	betrayal
justifying	rejection
ignoring	unloved
changing the subject	untrustworthy
pacifying	lonely
accepting	misunderstood
agreeing	hopeless

How to Parent the Child Inside

Not one of us grew to adulthood having *all* our needs gratified. You can develop your own inner nurturing parent to make up for what you feel that you missed as a child.

Close your eyes. See an image of yourself as a child. Let's say it's a boy. Ask the child to come over and sit on your lap. Tell the child how much you love him and how you want to give him what he feels that he wants from you. For example: "It's okay, honey. I will always take care of you. I will feed you and pick out your clothes for you and help you learn how to be strong and warm and fun-loving. I will stand behind you and support you against all opposition until you decide that you want to do that for yourself."

As you imagine this scene, you will discover what the child in you wanted from your parent and didn't get. You can learn how to give to yourself now.

EXPLORING BEHAVIOR

This activity will help you observe stock responses so that you can be free to change them.

- Many of us develop stock responses in relationships. Write about some of your stock responses. For example:

    Running My Number

    Everyone runs a number once in a while.
    When I do my number, I act in a way that isn't me.
    I pretend to care when I don't care at all
    Or I pretend not to care when I care a lot.
    Doing a number is putting on airs, creating an impression.

    Maybe I'm afraid people won't like me as I am
    So it's like being before an audience, trying hard to be something else.
    Some people run their number every time they meet another person.
    It's like getting into costume and walking out on a stage.
    It's like ordering a meal in a foreign language, or doing the wine-tasting trip with a waiter.
    Sometimes it's fun to run my number.
    But people who run a number in a relationship make it less real, put distance between people.
    When I see myself running my number, I can stop it.

- What roles do you play? For example: "I'm a nice guy." "I'm nurturing and protective." "I'm friendly and nice to be with." "I'm efficient and organized (no nonsense please—time is of the essence)."

- What roles do your friends and relatives play? Name a person. Let's say it's a woman. Write out her role, her act, or her "number." Write a description which includes the language she uses, her body movements and gestures, and her actions.

- Questions to explore about behavior: If a woman does a kind act is she therefore kind? If a man fights bravely is he therefore brave? What is the relationship between what a person says and what he does?

- How do you feel when someone says one thing and does another? Give examples of times when you said one thing and did another.

CHANGING BEHAVIOR

Our belief systems often limit our world. We spend energy defending what we believe in and making it fit our lives. On the other hand, a *working premise* is an idea to use as if it were true for the moment. You don't have to believe it. But assuming that you *can* do something results in a correspondence between consciousness and life. When you experience this connection, you can begin to change your behavior. As a working premise, let us assume that the following techniques work:

Behavior modification: Set up an experiment to get rewards for behavior you want. Be specific about the description of the behavior and the reward; the process must be recorded on a chart.

Guided imagery: Take fifteen minutes each day to relax in a quiet place and imagine some behavior you want to change. Visualize in detail the situation and the people involved (if any). Then watch yourself acting out the behavior you want.

Autosuggestion: Write down a few sentences about behavior you want to improve. Tell yourself how you are in the process of improving, step by step. Give yourself suggestions about the process of behavior change.

A good way to start changing unproductive behavior is to start setting goals for yourself. Your goals must be *realistic and achievable.* They must be based on your time, energy, and ability. Moreover, they must be *specific and measurable:* I will lose two pounds next week. And, finally, your goals must be based on *motivation and intention.* Some goals take longer to achieve than others. Write down your goals and record your progress step by step. Write how it feels to reach a goal:

I have experienced satisfaction in . . .

I felt successful when . . .

I achieved . . .

SETTING GOALS

To reach goals you must know what you want and state exactly what you intend to achieve. Many of your choices today will determine whether or not you will get where you want to go.

- Make a list of goals: athletics, art, music, degrees, job, social activities, finances, relationships.

- Select one of these goals and explain why it is important to you.

- Write down what you will have to do to reach that goal. For example: quit smoking, get more sleep, quit your job, stop watching TV.

- Make a list of five goals to reach this year. List steps to reach each of these goals.

- Write down five goals you wish to reach in five years. List the steps necessary to reach those goals.

- Some needs are more important than others. List your goals in order of importance. Make a schedule of short-term, mid-term, and long-term goals (see chart).

- Change the statement "I can reach my goal" to "I *will* reach my goal." Watch your behavior. It will tell you what you really value.

YOUR HABITS

> *We are what we repeatedly do.*
> *Excellence, then, is not an act*
> *but a habit.*
>   *Aristotle*

Productive habits are useful and save time. Unproductive habits can be changed. Mark Twain said "Habit is habit, and not to be flung out of the window by any man; but coaxed downstairs a step at a time." Although behavior can be resistant to change, it can be modified depending upon our intentions.

- Do you have a way of behaving that you want to change? Describe that behavior in very specific ways. Step by step tell about it. Give several examples of it.

- If you are either uncomfortable or dissatisfied with an action or behavior, how would you like to behave?

- One way to change behavior is through imagination. You can change your behavior by concentrating, relaxing, and visualizing the way you want to act. Close your eyes and relax. In your imagination, act out in detail the kind of behavior you want. Notice how your body moves. Look at the expressions on your face. Step by step go through the process of behaving in the way you want. Practice in your imagination several times a day. While you are doing some automatic task (shaving, washing the dishes, dressing), visualize the behavior you want. Practice this change at least twice a day for two weeks until it becomes a habit. Write about your progress. Then reward yourself with something special. By setting goals, visualizing, acting out the changes, and rewarding yourself, you can become more like the person you want to be. Cary Grant said, "I pretended to be someone I wanted to be, and finally I became that person."

A Typical Goal Chart

	Personal growth	Education	Job	Family	Possessions	Health	Spiritual life	Experiences
Short-term goals								
Mid-term goals								
Long-term goals								

Part Three

Communicating With Others

Recently scientists found evidence of life many billions of years ago. Perhaps life is eternal, without beginning or end, constantly transformed into some new state. Yet no other organism can compare to humans. The human brain and communication systems are without equal and create such great changes in the world that we leave it a very different place from the world we entered. As voyagers, we search with both fear and delight to find what lies around the corner.

Part Three examines relationships, for in our search we join hands to explore together in order to play our part in this evolutionary process. Both individually and collectively, we can learn to expand our human potential. Our dreams must exceed our grasp if we are to transcend our present state. Therefore, we explore the processes of transition and growth.

The expression, "I feel like a new person!" illustrates the universal experience of rebirth. We experience profound crises, ordeals, suffering, and loss from which we often experience death and resurrection. Each of us at times sees our life as a failure. This feeling comes from the vague knowledge that somehow we have not fulfilled our potential. We dream of life renewed. We are in fact capable of rebirth; of transmuting life. Such renewal comes from the hope of beginning life over again.

Every day is the first day of the rest of our lives. This time we will be more wise and live with more integrity. We want to make a difference in the world. This vision comes as we search for better ways to live, to expand our horizons and to gain greater awareness of ourselves in the world.

Shall we permit our fellow men to know us as we are, or shall we seek instead to remain an enigma, an uncertain quantity wishing to be seen as something we are not?

Sidney Jourard

10

Communicating in Relationships

We have explored communication as a process of creating meaning—perception, context, and self-concept. Getting to know ourselves gives us a solid basis for forming relationships with others. We communicate information about the self—personal perceptions, intentions, values, beliefs—whether we are aware of it or not. Rarely in life do we ask for or get honest responses about how we come across to others. Seldom do we enter relationships with the expressed agreement to give and receive feedback. Yet it is essential that we examine how we communicate in relationships.

Writing down our first impressions gives us a chance to compare our initial perceptions with later ones. We may find that we project our own traits, feelings, or reactions onto others who do not have them at all. We can find out the accuracy of them if we are willing to share them with others. Writing about others and ourselves in relationships can be fruitful. We learn about the accuracy of our perceptions when we share our impressions with others.

A baby begins life by bonding emotionally with its family—its first primary relationship and a complex, intimate, personal and social connection. As children develop, they include close, intimate friends in their primary relationship group. Later secondary relationships include acquaintances, neighbors, social friends, and co-workers. The theories, principles, and experiences of interpersonal relationships apply to all aspects of communication—personal, social, and public.

Moment by moment we create our perceptions of others as they create their perceptions of us. Research indicates that we start to make up our minds about other people within seven seconds of meeting them. Consciously or unconsciously, we signal our true feelings with our eyes, faces, bodies and attitudes. We trigger in each other a chain of emotional reactions ranging from approval to fear. If we communicate friendliness, energy, and interest in others, people will be attracted to us.

RELATIONSHIP SKILLS

Imagine yourself in a situation where you are alone . . . and you are offered one of the two, books or men . . . I do indeed, close my door at times and surrender myself to a book, but only because I can open the door again and see a human being looking at me.

Martin Buber

Although, many of us want to be around other humans for many reasons, some people are less interested or more selective about forming relationships. Because we often experience difficulty communicating with others, it helps to know that differences in sex, age, interests, and experiences influence relationships. Skills in initiating social experiences can be learned.

These questions can help you evaluate qualities that improve communication. Out of all the people you know:

- whom would you name as a warm, friendly person?
- who talks the most? who talks the least?
- who is the best listener?
- who contributes the most meaningful comments?
- who seems the most trusting and open?
- who seems to understand himself or herself the most?
- who seems the most effective in helping others?
- who understands others the most?

- who expresses himself or herself the most freely?
- who seems most able (and who least able) to accept negative or threatening remarks?
- who gets off the subject most often?
- who tries to be polite? who is the most aggressive?
- who analyzes the most (Uses "Why?" and "Because . . .")?
- who evaluates the most (good/bad, right/wrong, should . . .)?
- who uses the phrase "Yes, but . . ." the most?
- who is the most authentic, real person you know?

Now evaluate yourself on the social skills listed above.

Many social scientists tell us *humans are herd animals.* However individuals differ in the amount of time they want to spend with others. Social people are usually enthusiastic and enjoy others of all ages. They feel good if they can cheer up depressed friends. They smile when they speak to strangers or salesclerks. They have no difficulty starting a conversation and feel at ease in crowds and with strangers. They make friends easily. However, they often feel restless, even unhappy, if they have to spend too much time alone. The energy and stimulation they get from being with other people makes them feel alive.

In contrast, Henry David Thoreau wrote:

I love to be alone. I never found the companion that was as companionable as solitude. We are for the most part more lonely when we go abroad among men than when we stay in our chambers.

Being alone is *not* the same as being lonely. Loneliness is a basic sense of unrelatedness, or the compulsive longing for the impossible in a relationship with another person, or an unwillingness to accept one's own separateness. According to their own reports, adolescents suffer the most from loneliness, mature people outgrow loneliness, and people over sixty-five are less lonely than any other age group.

PERSONALITY DIFFERENCES

Carl Jung, a Swiss psychiatrist, developed theories of personality to help people understand their relationships to themselves and others. He believed humans developed two basic attitudes towards life—extraversion and introversion. The extravert's energy and interests flow outward toward external happenings—people, things, events. The introvert's energy and interests flow predominantly inward. The extravert gains energy from going to a party while the introvert gets drained.

Introverts need a considerable amount of solitude to develop their creativity. They enjoy their aloneness and develop a rich, inner life. They treasure their freedom and individuality. Although they enjoy people, they tend to have fewer friends. They often develop deep, long lasting friendships. Unlike the extravert who counts *numbers* of friends, the introvert measures quality of friendship—a deep, permanent relationship with a special person.

Do you see yourself as more extroverted (enjoy people) or more introverted (enjoy solitude)? Both states are desirable. More than half of the time:

- Are you social, outgoing, pleasant, cooperative; or do you often prefer to read a good book, write, paint, work on projects, plan, dream, and imagine your future?

- Do you get along with most people or are you drawn to relatively few people? Are you selective?

- Do you prefer spending time with one other person or with groups of people?

- Do you prefer to share personal problems with others, or do you protect your private thoughts and feelings?

- Do you like to be the center of attention or do you prefer to remain unnoticed?

- If another person tells a story, do you listen with empathy and interest or does your mind wander off to your own projects?

- Would others tend to ask you for help knowing you would drop everything or do people generally not ask you for help?

- Do you usually think about other people or does your mind dwell on projects and ideas?

- Do you tell your friends what you think of them or do you keep your judgments of others to yourself?

If, as a child, you tended to be social (restless when you were alone), you will usually tend to be social as an adult.

According to a survey, seventy-five percent of the general population tends to be extraverted while only twenty-five percent are reportedly introverted. Because our Western culture sanctions outgoing, sociable, and gregarious temperaments, introverts report going through much of their lives believing they "ought" to be more sociable. Their legitimate desires for space and time of their own, for private places in the mind and environment, may not be satisfied.

Another aspect of personality includes our individual modes of perception—different ways we perceive the world—from outer sensation or personal intuition. Sensory people are understood in terms of happiness/sadness, optimism/pessimism while intuitives are understood in terms of sensitivity/insensitivity and awareness/unawareness. The sensory person wants facts and believes in experience. Sensory people are realistic, down-to-earth, and practical. The intuitive person has hunches, is imaginative, hypothesizes about a situation, sees its possibilities, leaps to conclusions. Surveys indicate that seventy-five percent of us tend to perceive the world through the sensory modes while twenty-five percent prefer intuitive modes of perceiving reality. It is oftentimes the intuitives, judged as having their "heads-in-the-clouds", who make valuable contributions to scientific research and artistic forms.

A third aspect of personality includes our modes of judging our experiences—thinking or feeling. The thinking type tends to be objective and impersonal. The feeling person tends to be subjective and personal. Thinking people value principles, policy, law, firmness, justice, standards, and analysis. Feeling people prefer values, extenuating circumstances, intimacy, persuasion, harmony, sympathy, and devotion. Although six out of ten women make decisions based on feelings while six out of ten men prefer to make judgments based on logic, feeling/thinking is divided equally in the general population.

As individuals we differ in fundamental ways. We want different things and have different motives, purposes, aims, values, needs, drives, and impulses. We believe, think, perceive and understand differently. We tend to judge others as "wrong" or flawed if they are not like us, and spend our lives trying to change them to be more like us. Fortunately, sculpting others in our own likeness usually fails. If we can understand and value (not simply accept) our differences, we can greatly improve our ability to enjoy each other. When an intuitive person talks to a factual person or, an intellectual talks to someone who lives through feelings, communication can breakdown. When we understand that individuals have different attitudes toward life, different ways of perceiving, and different methods of judging the world, we can attempt to speak in a language the other person understands.

We tend to choose people who are like us for our friends. An extrovert can join a friend who wants to go to a party while an introvert can understand a friend's need for solitude. When like friends communicate, they empathize with and understand each other. In marriage, polar opposites attract and complement each other. For example, when a thinking man and a wife who judges through feelings appreciate their differing viewpoints, their cooperative efforts can be quite successful. Mates however, make the mistake of expecting their spouse's reactions, needs, and desires to be the same. This results in communication misunderstandings.

To create understanding relationships ask these questions:

- "How are you seeing this situation?"
- "What do you think/feel about it?"
- How would you solve this problem?"

We can learn to enjoy the values of differing personalities.

We can also learn to be more effective in solving our mutual problems and in our relationships as friends, co-workers, and partners.

SOCIAL EXPECTATIONS

In order to function, a society sets rules and teaches its members how to cooperate for the welfare of the group. Therefore, we have been taught certain values. Once we have been taught what is "good" and "bad" (right and wrong), we believe people "should" think, feel, and behave in those ways.

Write down examples of ways you believe people "should" behave

- People should . . .
- I should . . .
- My friends should . . .

Unrealistic and irrational expectations can interfere with our relationships. Which of these expectations do you have?

- People ought to trust me.
- I should be happy.
- Life should be fair.
- People shouldn't act the way they do.
- People should be punished for their errors.
- People should help everyone who needs it.
- I should never hurt people.
- Others have no right to hurt me.
- If people cared about me, they would do what I want.
- When I do things for others, they should appreciate it.

One way to feel miserable is to set unrealistic standards you or others cannot meet.

Words like "should/shouldn't", "right/wrong", "good/bad" indicate a tendency to be critical, hostile, rebellious or distrusting. When we are accepting, nonjudgmental, supportive, agreeable, trusting, caring, friendly, and sociable—people will move toward us.

Become aware of your communication habits:

- Describe a time when you simply listened without trying to give advice, agree, or sympathize. How did the person respond?

- Compare the times of simply listening with the times of verbalizing acceptance. Which felt best to you?

- Describe a time you said or did something that made someone feel really good.

Each of us is an individual and all of us are exposed to the same social pressures. We can design a system of reciprocal altruism in communicating to ensure better personal relationships.

KINDS OF RELATIONSHIPS

Never, never, for the sake of peace and quiet, deny your own experience.
Hammarskjold

Although we experience many different kinds and qualities of relationships, the first ones we learn are hierarchical. Hierarchy relationships are those in which power and control are unequal: parent/child, teacher/student, employer/employee. In hierarchy relationships, such as parent and child, caring may not always be reciprocated. In fact some degree of overt or covert hostility often accompanies unequal power relationships. In peer relationships two individuals share equal or comparable power and control. Some adults, more often women, continue to give away their power to others who consciously or unconsciously accept control. These unequal power adult relationships continue the manipulative tactics of childhood. In this chapter, we discuss peer relationships between friends and co-workers in which power, respect, and caring can be reciprocated and mutual.

Friendship

One man writes:

Friend is a lovely word; love (which is a component of friendship) is its only serious rival. . . . Everyone needs friends. We may do without lovers or wives or husbands. We may live a celibate and happy life, but none of us can do without friends. Friends are essential if we are to become and remain truly human.

Even experts don't agree on the meaning of friendship. Its many kinds and qualities make definitions and classifications difficult. "What is friendship?", and "What are its qualities?"

On a separate sheet of paper write about the different kinds of friendships you have or had:

- Convenience friends: next-door neighbors, car-poolers, parents whose children are friends, mutual aid friends

- Special interest friends: sports, politics, clubs, shopping

- Historical friends: friends from childhood or the past

- Crossroads friends: college roommates, first-job friends, service buddies, friends made while traveling, etc.

Other ways of classifying friends:

- By quality: surface, medium, close, and best friends

- By sex: same sex friends, opposite sex friends

- By age: cross-generational, younger, same age, older

Write about the kinds of friendships you have now or have had in the past to discover patterns that occur again and again.

Friendship Life Cycles

In the beginning, babies depend on adults to care for them to sustain life. But by the age of three to five, children make friends easily and grow more social. Then from five to twelve, quarreling among friends with some moments of cooperation are common. In the teens, peers become more important than family, and both sexes tend to socialize with groups of friends. Then dating begins. As single men and women search for partners, friends and peer groups are still important, but after marriage, the importance of friends declines. Generally adults depend less on peers or their opinions. In mid-life, as children leave the nest, friends may become important again. As friends and peers die, some people over sixty-five join senior social groups while others move into isolation. Health professionals encourage friendship for emotional well-being. Although many people do not know what they value, many want interaction with others.

What do you want from a friend?

- Someone to comfort me when I'm in trouble
- Someone who will listen without being critical
- Someone to share my successes and be glad for my triumphs
- Someone who can encourage me in my hours of defeat
- Someone to reflect back what I say and who I am
- Someone who can help me grow, change, and mature
- Someone who is reliable, loyal, trustworthy
- Someone who accepts me as I am

Notice that what you want from a friend changes over time—a primary reason why friendships end.

Ironically, this list of "wants" implies others will be the givers of support and caring while we will be the beneficiaries. Be aware that a degree of equity in need satisfaction is important.

What kind of a friend are you? Do you give what you want? Take out a piece of paper:

- Make a list of friends you have or have had.
- Under each name, write what you gave to that friend.
- Using the list of what you want from friends, make a list of what you give to your friends. Be specific. Give examples.

Add your personal "gifts" to this list.

Many of us tend to keep mental lists of things we do for others, but conveniently forget what others have done for us. Part of giving includes not keeping score and not expecting something in return. "Counting" to see that you get as much as you give lacks generosity. Notice "scorekeeping" tendencies.

You create your methods for developing friendships.

- Write about a friendship that is or was good.

- What makes it good? (Avoid rose-colored nostalgia.)

- Write about a "not so good" friendship.

- In what ways are these friendships different?

- Under what conditions have you avoided reaching out to others when you needed them?

- Do you sometimes resist others reaching out to you? (Examples.)

- What makes personal commitment so difficult?

- Have you tried to renew an old relationship? (Example.)

Close friendships may not be a priority at certain times in life.

Gender Differences

For men, traditionally, friendship rests on shared activities; for women, it rests on shared conversations. Men report that their best friend is often their wife; women report their best friend is usually another female. Male friendships are generally low-key and center around things they do together. Men tend to keep their friendships on a more surface level. In contrast, female friendships are usually more intense, more valued, more intimate, and more dependent than male friendships.

According to researchers, men's friendships are generally more durable than women's. Men seldom confront a friend whose attitudes or behavior bothers them. In contrast, women are often more critical of their friends and less satisfied with them than men. Women tend to be extremely sensitive to their friends' "flaws" and express their feelings even if it means losing the friend.

Friendship Has Its Price

The world is filled with people, but real friends are rare. Because we are vulnerable to disapproval, many of us search for the nurturing support of friends. Friendship is a fragile relationship and requires time, attention, energy, and caring. It is easier made than developed or maintained over time. It requires commitment, loyalty, consideration, empathy, generosity, thoughtfulness, and nurturing. We often find ourselves disillusioned by friendship because we expect too much of both ourselves and others. Like all relationships, friends experience guilt, resentment, anger, rejection, and sadness. Yet one older man says, "Without friends, you're like a book that nobody bothers to pick up".

Describe your friendships:

- How many good friends do you have? Too many or too few?

- Do you have a friend you no longer speak to? What happened?

- When you want to end a friendship, how do you do it?

- Have you ever felt that you were "dumped" by a friend?

- Have you been disillusioned by a friend? What did you want that you didn't get?

- Do you enjoy letting someone else make decisions?

- Do you control or let friends think they're in control?

- Did you ever get mad at a friend? What did you do about it? What did your friend do?

- Are you better at giving or getting criticism?

- How do you give criticism? (Examples.)

- How do you react to getting criticism? (Examples.)

Write descriptions of a few friendships and what you wanted. Notice that what you wanted may have changed as you changed.

In the hierarchy of values, family relationships usually come first because they are our primary source of love. The family nuclear unit takes much of our time, effort, and love. But eventually, most of us leave home. Thirty percent of men and twenty-three percent of women today have never married. Of those who marry, spouses divorce or die. In old age, we seldom live in a family unit. Today, a large percentage of Americans live alone. Thus after family, friendships offer emotional intimacy or companionship that enriches us.

In our fantasies, we imagine ideal friends who trust, care for, accept, support, and defend us. They act as mirrors allowing us to accept ourselves with our imperfections and allowing us to risk change. Our fantasy image of friendship includes free will, equity, trust, selflessness and affection. Friends also share values and goals. They hold common beliefs and support our views of the meaning of life. In reality, however, our friendship fantasies seldom live up to the ideal. We experience disappointment and pain when we expect perfection. We don't choose our parents or our children, but we choose our friends. Today, as more people choose to remain single, friendships often become our primary relationships.

Friendships End

A friendship has a birth, a life, and a death. We expect most romantic relationships to end and accept that half of all marriages end in divorce, but we have no statistics for lost friendships. We want intimacy or companionship or someone to go places with. But as we change, so does what we want from friends. Feeling guilty or rejected, we make up excuses for letting friendships lapse. Individual interests, priorities, and life styles are not static. As we change, friendships fade. With the end of a friendship, some people experience the pain of divorce.

Write about a friendship that seemed to outgrow its usefulness.

- A friend was so successful that you backed away. He (she) reminds you of what you haven't accomplished. Around him (her) you feel inferior. Or you are successful. Your friend withdrew. Or you find you want to be with other "winners."

- People move. Distance can kill a friendship.

- Interests change. Your friend (or you) stayed single while the other married and/or has a family.

- A friend develops an irritating habit (drinking, smoking . . .) or attitude (possessiveness, dependence on you, envy . . .) that you find impossible to tolerate.

- Your friend subtly demands more and more from you in time, attention or support. You feel guilty (anxious, confused . . .) if you don't include this person in everything you do. As you change and grow, you meet new people with different interests.

- You find you no longer want to tell your friend your secrets. The loss of intimacy may come from a lack of understanding or some disagreement over values or beliefs, but you no longer trust your friend for the emotional support you want.

- For some reason, you have begun to feel angry, resentful, betrayed, or other unpleasant emotions around this friend.

- Write from your personal experience about losing a friend.

We can find graceful ways of ending relationships. We can sense when we or our friends begin to become defensive or withdrawn. Although friendships end, we can let go without guilt or anger.

Support Networks

In times of stress—a death in the family, a divorce, a family argument, work or financial problems (losing a job or a promotion, trouble with a boss . . .) we need emotional support. Friends, neighbors and family members can sometimes assist us in coping with temporary emotional and/or physical problems.

What kind of a support network do you have?

How many neighbors do you trade favors with? (Water plants, loan tools, share rides, babysitting, etc. . . .)

At work, how many persons do you talk to about personal problems?

Do you live with someone you can talk to?

How often do you visit with friends or close family members?

How many people do you talk to about personal matters?

How often do you participate in a social or community group?

A personal burden may be too heavy for a vulnerable friendship. A friend may not have the time, energy, or experience to support you. At times, caring about a friend means not overloading them with your serious personal problems. In some cases, they are unequipped to handle severe, long-term or insoluble tragedies. In these cases, we can turn to support groups such as those listed with community social services. Substance abuse, divorce, Alzheimer's, and cancer groups are a few examples.

Although support groups serve emergencies, personal friendship is by its nature more authentic and freer of deceit than any other intimate relationship. It is a relationship less driven by sexual pleasure, money, power, promises of duty or the commitments of a marriage. The human need for friendship provides us with the opportunity to become more caring, selfless, affectionate human beings. With friends we can strive to become the most authentic, ethical individuals we have the capacity to become. Friendship gives value to personal survival.

Communicating at Work

Freud said that all humans have two great capacities—to love and to work. Some individuals displace a need for recognition through work with an insatiable hunger to be loved. Others have a stronger need to be recognized than to love or be loved. Today most of us yearn for work that is meaningful, expresses our creativity, or enriches us in some way.

At work, we communicate with bosses and co-workers. Any relationship functions best as it moves toward equality and a process of mutualism. An authoritarian, hierarchical, superior or expert relationship is ultimately unsatisfying—perhaps more for the boss than for the worker. People who work together rarely have the time to give each other feedback as equals. It's not always considered an acceptable social practice. However most of us want to learn how others perceive and evaluate us. If we want feedback, we can ask for it.

Explore your feelings and thoughts about your work:

- List three or four things you like most about your job.

- List three or four things you like least about your job.

- List three or four things you feel you do well in your job.

- List three or four things you feel you need to improve.

- List some things you do in your job that feel effortless.

- List some things that require a great deal of effort.

- In doing your job, when do you feel the most satisfied?

After answering these questions you can choose what you want to share with others at work.

We can increase our motivation and job satisfaction and learn to create more fulfillment in our work life in spite of the environment, nature of the work, or persons with whom we work.

Communication Skills at Work

A satisfying work relationship is directly affected by how well we communicate. The next exercise gives suggestions.

Identify your current strengths and areas for growth by rating the following elements from 1 (weak) to 5 (superior):

- I am aware of my feelings: anxiety, frustration, resentment, etc.
- When the source of negative feelings is connected with my job, I explore the "real" sources of those feelings.
- I try to verbalize a specific problem, defining my terms and giving concrete examples.
- I understand how my attitudes, beliefs, values, and feelings affect what I say and do.
- I carefully choose an appropriate time to communicate a problem.
- I ask for time to describe, define, and work out problems if I can not solve them by myself.
- I carefully word what I mean to say—avoiding judgments, accusations, and defense-producing language.
- I try to establish a problem solving atmosphere without manipulating others to get what I want.
- I am willing to compromise to solve conflicts.
- I bring a positive attitude to discussions.
- I believe open communication and shared feelings are valuable.
- I am willing to take the time to clarify my ideas and focus on issues (not persons).
- I am willing to accept suggestions and make choices.

- I am willing to allow time for changes to take place.

This exploration can lead to valuable improvements at work.

For positive language skills use the "I" point of view: "I have difficulty with . . .", "I am struggling with . . .", "I don't feel comfortable with . . .".

Problem Solving

On a separate sheet of paper describe a problem you are presently having at work. Give some concrete examples of this difficulty. For example:

- Jobs that are difficult, disagreeable, or cause you problems
- Bottlenecks that cause delays
- Jobs that require too many people
- Jobs that require a lot of chasing around
- Work that could be done outside the company for less
- Reports, forms, or records requiring necessary work
- Machines and equipment that are idle much of the time
- Operations that could be combined to save time
- Jobs that could be rescheduled to eliminate peaks or idle time
- Improper or inaccurate forms
- Jobs where quality of work is unsatisfactory
- Work duplicated by different departments

Writing and thinking about these issues can produce improvements.

When you give what you want from others—full attention and respect—your work relationships will improve.

Intimate Relationships

Although we will only briefly touch upon the subject of intimacy, every exercise in this journal can be used in a modified form to communicate in close relationships. The level of emotional involvement and commitment is often higher in intimate relationships than in other types of relationships.

Liking, affection, and love can be communicated.

- Make a list of people you like. Do you show them or tell them you like them? What behaviors show that you like them?

- Make a list of people you feel affection for. What behaviors (actions or words) show your affection for others?

- List different kinds of love and order the list in importance. For example: self-love, parental love, erotic love, love for a friend, sibling, mate, love of one's work, country, God . . .

- Write a personal definition of the three most important kinds of love in your life. Then give examples and describe them.

- How do you tell or show others you love them? Ask them if these are the ways they want to be loved.

LOVE

Passion cannot be beautiful without excess.
When one does not love too much,
one does not love enough.
                                Pascal

People use language to communicate experience. When people talk about being in love, whether they use the same definition or not, they are talking about a common experience. There are many kinds of love: brotherly love, love of mankind, parental love, love of God, marital love, romantic love. The most difficult kind of love to define is romantic love.

There is no human experience which is dreamed about with such great expectations and yet fails so regularly as romantic love. When two people allow themselves to feel close, however, and feel this moment of oneness, it becomes one of the most exhilarating experiences in life. If we have the courage and the strength, many of us experience love more than once in our lives. We might even learn that it is possible to love more than one person equally and fully at the same time. Friendship, affection, interest in others—all seem powerless beside the experience of love.

LOVING AND LOSING

The word LOVE *has a different meaning and is a different experience for each of us. These questions and suggestions are designed to clarify what loving means to you.*

- What is your definition of love? Write as many definitions as you can. Ask a person you love to define the word for you, and share your definition.

- Write about a love experience you have had or wish to have. How do you feel when you tell someone "I love you?" Give a specific example. How do you feel when someone tells you "I love you?" Write about a specific example.

- Write about the end of a love affair. How did you feel? How did you act? How did you react to the other person? How do you stop being in love? How do you feel when it's over?

One philosopher believes that we cannot love someone we *need*. If we feel as if our survival depends upon another person, then we cannot love them. He says that love is accepting others exactly as they are without wanting them to change. Love allows people to change if and when they want to change. When you need someone to be different than they are for your sake, then you do not love that person. When you need to make others wrong for being who they are, you do not love them.

The experience of love is created by the lover. It is difficult to measure the magnitude, intensity, quality, and durability of love. Yet when two lovers' affection and commitment to one another expand at approximately the same rate, they tend to reinforce their love. Such mutually reinforced love may not last forever, though. "If two people love each other," Hemingway observed, "there can be no happy end to it."

INTIMACY

Intimacy results from expressing warmth, tenderness, and closeness to others. Openly expressing affectionate feelings appropriately *and* sensitively *can result in intimate relationships.*

- In this past week, have you revealed yourself or let go of feelings or thoughts to another person? Write about such an experience.

- Notice when you are wearing a mask or playing a role with another person. Replace the role with consciously choosing to be open and authentic. Write about this experience.

- Write about a time when you were open and risked intimacy and the other person didn't respond. Was the situation appropriate? Were you sensitive to the mood of the other person?

- Write about a time when you risked being open and intimate and the other person did respond.

- Is intimacy with others one of your goals? Do you value intimacy? Under what conditions? With whom?

THE LITTLE THINGS

In an intimate relationship, it may not be the big things that cause a strain. Little things can pull two people apart.

- Give as many examples as you can of petty behavior that bothers you. For example: hogging the bathroom, coming home late again without calling, forgetting to say thank you.

- Write a list of little things that are important to you. For example: kissing goodnite, touching gently, having a place you can go and be accepted.

- How do you want others to show their love for you? Have you told them?

The kinds and qualities of love we want from another changes as an intimate relationship moves from romance to serious commitment. Making a marriage work is more complex than finding two people who have marriage potential. Those who plan to get married would benefit by telling each other why they want to be married.

I want to be married because I want:

- someone to love who will love me
- someone to share my life with
- someone to have children with and who will help me raise them
- someone I can take care of who will take care of me
- someone who will be a companion and friend
- someone who will eat, sleep, go places and do things with me, so I won't be lonely
- someone who will satisfy my physical/sexual needs

Think about your own reasons for wanting to be married.

Three common "wrong" reasons for marrying are 1) to acquire a regular sex partner, 2) to obtain economic or emotional security, and 3) to escape loneliness. A person who marries to escape unpleasant situations rarely experiences an enduring or satisfying marriage. A critical element in finding a marriage partner is "timing." The "right time" to be married differs for different persons.

"At this time in my life am I ready to:
- take on the responsibilities of marriage."
- be considerate of another person's feelings."
- help another person reach his or her goals."
- settle down to some degree of stability."
- make a permanent commitment to one person."
- be responsible to and for another person."
- handle the finances of marriage."

Ask yourself if you are able to follow through on each of the above statements.

If both individuals are amenable to marriage, if they want to be married for the right reasons, and if *now* is the right time in their lives for marriage, then marriage expectations can be discussed.

Role Expectations

A woman often wants a man who, without ever being asked, will carry out the garbage, help with the housework, run errands, and share her interests. She wants a man who not only helps with the baby but will take some responsibility for remembering when the baby needs to be changed and fed without being reminded. Similarly, a man will have personal expectations of his wife.

Some questions for discussion include:
- What kind of a marriage do I want?
- What kinds of roles do I want to take in a marriage?
- What do you expect of me, and what do I expect of you?

These questions should be discussed before marriage and again in later years since what we want and expect changes over time.

Marriage role expectations differ according to the stage of a marriage. A married couple often has the most difficulty during transitions from one stage of a marriage to another. The first year of a marriage is a different stage with different problems than the fifth to the tenth year, for example.

Characteristics of Marriage

Researchers have questioned thousands of married couples, asking them to define characteristics of an ideal husband and wife. Husbands and wives are not blind to each other's faults. Aware of the flaws in their mates and in themselves, they acknowledge rough times; but they believe that the likable qualities are more important than the deficiencies and the difficulties. "He isn't perfect," said one wife, "But I don't worry about his weak points. His strong points overcome them."

The purpose of this list is to provide an information exchange as to how each person perceives their self and their mate. First rate yourself, then rate your spouse. 5) Excellent, 4) above average, 3) average, 2) below average, 1) doesn't display this characteristic.

- He/she shares my interest and is my companion
- He/she listens, encourages, and comforts me
- He/she shares inner feelings, thoughts, fears, and dreams
- He/she is an attractive sexual partner
- He/she works and contributes to the family financially
- He/she cares for the children's physical and emotional needs
- He/she serves as a model of men/women for the children
- He/she helps manage the family income and finances
- He/she shares work and puts energy into making our home and surroundings attractive and comfortable
- He/she practices the family religion and philosophy

The ability to love, to communicate, to be intimate, to share interests, to listen with attention and respect for each other—our capacity for some of these may fade somewhat over time. If we enter a relationship with realistic expectations, we are less likely to be disappointed. Expecting later stages of a relationship to be like the beginning can only result in disillusionment.

Information Sharing

The following statements can serve as starting points for a discussion. First each partner separately reads the statements and briefly jots down words or thoughts to share. It is important that neither intends to change the other—the object is the sharing of information without demands or expectations. When possible, share information you have not previously discussed.

Tell your spouse:

- How satisfied you are with the part you presently play in your marriage—from 1 (low) to 10 (high)
- How you wish your marriage were different
- Three things you most enjoy and appreciate about him/her
- Three things you have difficulty dealing with about him/her
- Something you want that you are not getting
- Your fondest memory of your time together
- Your most painful memory
- Your greatest conflict in your marriage
- What his/her best and worst habits are
- What she/he did that made you feel sad (angry, happy)
- What he/she did that was a pleasant surprise
- Now tell each other something that you feel is important but that you haven't previously shared

The amount and kind of love we express through our actions may be as simple as "always being there" even in the form of being taken for granted—knowing that we can always count on the other person. "Love is in the eye of the beholder."

ENDING RELATIONSHIPS

Endings can be painful. To end an intimate relationship, even a dead one, can be so painful that many people choose to keep up an unproductive sham rather than move on. A child is born into a family and stays in that family for fifteen to twenty years. After a year or more in and out of relationships, marriage often follows. Most of us do not know how to live alone, to be alone, to exist without a relationship. We ask ourselves: How can I stand to be alone? Does it mean that I am unlovable if I cannot find someone to be with? Will I ever find anyone else? Perhaps I'd be better off staying with this person after all. What will happen to me if I get sick? If I die?

Some people stay in a relationship that is dissatisfying, boring, and unproductive simply because they are afraid to be alone. They may be afraid, moreover, that they are not good enough for anyone to want them. They move from one failing relationship to another. The failure in these relationships is not in their ending but in their inception. They are born by two individuals who have sold themselves short and settled for less than they wanted because they were afraid to be alone. Such a relationship has no future; its death is inevitable. Deciding that you do not have to settle for something less than what you want can result in more fulfilling relationships. You deserve a caring, sharing, mutually accepting relationship that can help both parties realize their potential.

The paradox is that being alone can be less lonely than being with someone when the relationship is unfulfilling. Being together can be lonelier, in fact, than being alone. All relationships must end. Choosing an ending is not a failure. You did not fail if you ended a relationship at its point of diminishing returns. To know that point is an art, however. Part of the good-bye process is leaving safety and routine for change—and the unknown can be fearful or exciting, depending upon what you choose.

LEAVING

Take some time to write about how you end relationships.

- How do you handle endings? How do other people handle them? Write some descriptions in detail.

- Some people settle for a relationship that is boring or unsatisfying rather than be alone. What other choices do you have? Write out some statements to ponder. For example: I can cut off any relationship that freezes me into patterns. Perhaps the kind of life I want may be possible only if I am single. I can find a partner who intends to create with me the kind of relationship I want.

Our intimate relationships often give us the most joy and the most pain. Sometimes we have difficulty expressing love, caring, and intimacy. Sometimes we are frightened of being dependent on others or of having them be dependent on us. An interdependent relationship often means balancing between being close and being free. Yet two people rarely coordinate these individual needs so that both people want to be close or free at the same time.

Moreover, few of us want the same degree of commitment as our partner in a relationship. Yet commitments and agreements are made—usually unconsciously. Commitments change and commitments end. Few of us know how to handle change and endings. Through the process of communication we can learn to relate to others in more satisfying ways.

> *We arrive upon this earth alone.*
> *We depart alone.*
> *This time called life was meant to share.*
> Walter Rinder

Humans are so complex, no one aspect of life defines us unless we choose to be defined by it. The primary "tags" people use to define themselves are sex, age, work, income, status, race, and religion. As we mature, we learn that we choose our own definitions and values. This discovery gives us *the ultimate freedom of self-definition*. In chapter 11, we will explore additional suggestions for expanding the process of relating to others by breaking through barriers to communication.

Every act of birth requires the courage to let go of something . . . to let go eventually of all uncertainties, and to rely only upon one thing: one's own power to be aware and to respond; that is one's own creativity.

Fromm

11

Communication Barriers

Once we develop relationships, we often want to expand them and continue them. Certain barriers to communication can occur in every relationship, however. Finding out what these are, learning how to cope with them, and discovering ways of resolving interpersonal conflict can result in growth and personal satisfaction.

Communication problems will always be with us, especially the defense mechanisms we use to hide from ourselves. We also need to know the ways we put others on the defensive. Identifying and resolving conflicts can help us develop more effective ways of communicating and relating.

In this chapter we will begin to integrate all the separate aspects we have studied: language, mind, body, emotions, and behavior in relationship with the self and others. The process of synthesis is essential to communication and occurs continuously. Each of us would benefit by developing a personal list of effective steps in communicating and relating.

The journal provides you with the opportunity of reviewing, redefining, and reexperiencing some of the key concepts we have been dealing with. Integrating communication, expanding relationships, and exploring personal growth can all be accomplished through the communication journal.

CHECKLIST OF COMMUNICATION PROBLEMS

Read this list and choose three items that represent communication barriers for you. Transform each into a personal goal for improving your ability to communicate.

1. Failure to listen or to allow the other person to talk
2. Failure to observe nonverbal cues of others (actions, symbols, signs, gestures, mannerisms, sounds, and other signals)
3. Failure to *give* nonverbal cues (or appropriate ones)
4. Failure to allow for differences in perception (differences in education, age, culture, speed of thinking)
5. Failure to use a precise vocabulary that can be understood (being vague, using technical jargon, using abstractions without specific examples)
6. Failure to take enough time to complete a discussion or clarify questions both asked and answered

ATTITUDE

Communication is a form of loving. Write some observations of your communication. When do you "turn off" or "tune out?" We cannot always take enough time to listen to others and clarify communication. To improve communication takes time and energy. But most of all it takes honesty. When you can't listen because you do not have the time or energy, state those facts in some kind, accepting way: "I have something troubling me at the moment and I am having difficulty listening." "I am feeling some irritation and anxiety. I am afraid I will miss an appointment." "I am feeling distracted. I'm concerned about my little boy."

COMMUNICATION BREAKDOWN

Communication breakdowns occur when we are unaware of language differences caused by context variations.

- Without judging, write about a misunderstanding you have observed or experienced. Then analyze the misunderstanding. How could it have been avoided or cleared up?

- Start a diary of misunderstandings that you experience. Use such headings as:

    Barriers to understanding: age, sex, race, background, education

    Differences in: beliefs, attitudes, values, assumptions, moods

    Language: choice of words, precision, connotation, denotation, level of abstraction

    What patterns do you notice in your misunderstandings?

- Describe a communication breakdown to another person. If you want feedback, ask for it. When you receive feedback, do not justify or explain; simply say "Thank you." What did the feedback teach you?

By acknowledging the complexities of the communication process, we can begin to understand why we have communication problems. When we tell someone "You are wrong," we are saying "I see it differently than you do." Beginning with an acknowledgment of differences in perception, we can expand our awareness of misunderstandings. We can learn to restate, question, expand, explain, and clarify both what we say and what we hear.

SELF-DECEPTION

Theoretically, at least, the more we share with others the more they can reflect back to us the images we project. Yet none of us will ever be totally free of self-deception. Self-deception is a universal human problem. We simply cannot believe everything we say. To illustrate this problem, here are some incongruities that may occur because of self-deception. According to surveys, a large percentage of people say they detest sex and violence on television; yet programs with sex and violence do well in the TV ratings. Shoppers say that advertised products are better than house brands; yet they buy the house brand more often than advertised products. People say that personal appearance is not important in relationships; yet people at a dance picked the most attractive people as their choice for a future date.

Clearly there is a discrepancy between what people say are their values and how they actually act. The hidden meanings in our responses are for the most part unconscious or unknown. In self-deception the liar and the one lied to are one and the same. Therefore, it often takes another person to help us discover our own self-deceptions—to find whatever we are protecting ourselves from seeing or knowing. Self-deception affects the quality of our communicating and relating.

DEFENSE MECHANISMS

Your body will tell you when you are reacting defensively. Your muscles will tense up; your skin will sweat or heat up; your heart rate will increase. Here are some common defense mechanisms:

Repression: Unconscious forgetting or simply inhibiting any threatening stimuli—"I forgot my dentist appointment."

Projection: Attributing one's own faults, thoughts, or desires to others; projecting guilt on them—"My father is stingy." (I'm afraid that I'm stingy.)

Rationalization: Finding reasons other than the real one to make actions, thoughts, or words acceptable to the self-image—"Everybody cheats."

Withdrawal: Daydreaming to escape reality, pain, responsibility, or decisions; inability to get things done—"People don't care about me, so I'd rather be alone."

Compensation: Substituting achievement in one area to make up for weakness in another—"I'm homely so I try to get good grades."

Identification: Establishing a oneness with a valued person, group, or thing—"I belong to group X and that makes me important."

Displacement: Disguising a wish (fear or hate) by substituting another object to blame—the wife takes out her feelings against her husband on the child (and the child kicks the dog).

Regression: Resorting to behavior that is characteristic of an earlier age—"I'm going home to mother."

Reaction formation: Exaggerating the opposite of true feelings—"We've got to wipe out pornography" (enjoys pornography).

Aggression: Hurting and attacking oneself or others either verbally or physically—"The best defense is a good offense."

These are just a few classic defense mechanisms. Defensiveness damages communication and relationships. Judging, controlling, blaming, manipulating, acting superior—all put others on the defense.

DEFENSIVE COMMUNICATION

We can learn to identify and modify defensive communication in ourselves and others.

- For one week, keep a defensiveness diary. Write down the times you felt defensive and the times someone else was being defensive with you. For each entry, ask yourself:

    1. Was some judgment made?
    2. Was there an attempt to control or manipulate?
    3. Were there hidden motives?
    4. Was there a lack of concern or caring?
    5. Was there an attitude of superiority?
    6. Was there an attitude of dogmatic certainty?

JUDGING OTHERS

Bertrand Russell talked about "irregular verbs." His point was that we use complimentary words for judging ourselves, neutral words for the person we are speaking with, and negative words for an absent third party. Complete the following table:

I	You	He
I am righteously indignant.	You are annoyed.	He makes a fuss about nothing.
I am sparkling.	You are talkative.	He makes a drunken scene.
I am flexible.		
I respect my parents.		
I am a liberal.		
I have high moral principles.		
I'm a trifle overweight.		
I choose friends carefully.		
I am slender.		
I avoid fighting.		

CONFLICT RESOLUTION

If you and I decide that we have a problem (it's not your problem or my problem), then we can set up a time to work it out and discuss it. Write it out first. List the things that are bothering you. List the things you appreciate and enjoy about the other person. Get together and read each other's lists. Here are some steps to guide you:

1. Describe the problem, define it in detail, and give examples. Let the other person read what you have written. Ask him or her to repeat it back. Before going on, be sure both parties agree on the definition of the problem. If either of you is unwilling to find a solution, feel free to say so. If both parties are willing to go on, then go to step 2.

2. Write out as many solutions as you can think of. Try not to rely on traditional solutions. Be as creative and original as you can. Take time. Let your suggestions sit. Then agree to another meeting. *Warning:* Your suggestions are merely suggestions. You are not bringing solutions to your next meeting. You do not have to defend your suggestions.

3. Which of these solutions seems best? In a discussion, keep tossing solutions around without persuading or manipulating. Are you free to allow the other person to decide which solution he or she wants? If not, say so. Write down one solution that you both agree upon.

4. Try it out. Assume it will work. Trust each other. If one person fails to do what you have agreed, talk about it. Can you allow for occasional lapses? Avoid criticism. Decisions are never final.

5. Revise or modify solutions. Try something else. New information may lead to redefining the problem. Many times problems change. Sometimes people change.

Not all conflicts can be resolved. Not all problems have solutions. You can agree to disagree and find some way to live with your disagreements. No one you ever meet will have all the same beliefs and values you have. If you are unwilling to compromise, perhaps you would prefer to live alone. Many people find living alone comfortable. They have friends, work, relatives they love and enjoy; but they don't feel they have to live with someone. One young woman said: "The kind of life I want can only be lived as a single person."

Skills in conflict resolution take practice. Identify, discuss, and clarify the problem. Look behind the specific behavior to get to the feeling behind the conflict. Do you like to fight? One student said: "I like a good fight. When I get angry, I release tension. I don't need to change the other person; I just want someone who can allow me to blow off steam and not take it personally."

DEALING WITH CONFLICT

Identifying individual patterns of conflict can help us develop new and more effective ways of communicating.

- Recall the last three conflicts you have had—the most recent ones—with people who were important to you. Describe each conflict. What was it all about? What happened? How did you react? How did the other person react? How did the conflict end? What were the results? How did you feel? How did the other person feel? Do you want to continue resolving conflicts in these ways? Does the result make you feel better than before? Does your relationship get stronger?

- Do you have a pattern for dealing with conflict?

- Have you ever hit someone or been hit as a result of a disagreement? How do you feel about the incident now? Is your pattern of conflict working for you? Do you want to change your conflict patterns?

- Give an example of a time when someone blew off steam with you or responded all out of proportion to the situation. Can you give an example of a time when you could allow another person to get angry without taking it personally or defending yourself? How does that feel? What happens to the conflict when you don't respond with defensiveness?

THE DOUBLE BIND

When one party has power over another (parent/child, doctor/patient) and then denies that power and pretends equality, both the victim and the victimizer are locked in a double-bind situation. To be aware of these paradoxical communications can prevent some of them. Strategies, games, and double binds are patterns of interpersonal communication that involve incongruent messages. Thus the communicator, in effect, denies the message.

- Can you think of some double binds? For example: the father who wants obedience but says "Call me by my first name. Don't think of me as your dad, I want to be your buddy."

- Make a list of double-bind commands. For example: "Be spontaneous!" "Love me!" "Be independent!" "Grow up!"

EVALUATING YOUR COMMUNICATION SKILLS

Answer the following questions:

1. Are you usually able to say what you are trying to say?

2. When you do not understand something another person says, do you usually ask a question or ask for an explanation or example?

3. When you talk, do others often put words in your mouth?

4. Do you often check out whether others really know what you are saying?

5. Do you often ask others how they feel about what you are saying?

6. Is it difficult for you to talk with other people?

7. What topics do you usually talk about?

8. How do you check out whether those topics are of interest to the other person?

9. If someone else is talking about something of little interest to you, what do you do?

10. When your ideas differ from those around you, what do you do?

11. Are you able to put yourself in the other person's place? How often?

12. Are you aware of your tone of voice?

13. Are you aware of how it affects others?

14. When you have something to say that will hurt the other person, what do you do?

15. When someone else tells you something that sounds critical, what do you experience? What do you do?

16. If you feel hurt, do you tell the other person?

17. When someone disagrees with you, how do you feel? What do you do?

18. When you are angry, can you think clearly? Do you like to fight?

19. Do you avoid saying anything that will make the other person angry?

20. How do you settle differences (conflicts) with others?

IT'S OKAY TO BE IMPERFECT

Make a list of your shortcomings. For example:

1. *I sometimes deceive myself.* (It's okay to have areas of self-deception. There are no easy answers. I will always have parts of myself that are unknown.)

2. *I create definite images of myself with words that lock me in.* (It's okay to create a self-image knowing the words are not who I am.)

3. *I am often emotionally ambivalent.* (It's okay to feel what I feel; to want to be close to another person yet free; to want to make a commitment but be free to break it if it gets destructive or unfulfilling.)

4. *I am sometimes inconsistent.* (It's okay to say one thing and do another. It sometimes helps to talk about the way I want to act even when I have not yet become that person all the time.)

5. *I have conflicting values.* (It's okay to want things both ways at the same time.)

6. *I expect more of myself, my friends, and my relationships than any of us can possibly live up to.* (It's okay to have high expectations. Sometimes they can help me reach a higher level of achievement.)

INTEGRATING COMMUNICATION

To review our communication behaviors can help us synthesize what we have experienced.

- Recall a time when you really communicated. Write about it.

- Recall a time when you didn't communicate. Write about it.

- Write about a time when someone didn't communicate with you.

- Recall a time when you were listening and not liking it.

- Recall pretending to listen. What did you do?

- Recall talking and feeling nothing was communicated.

- Write about a time when you felt communicating was not worthwhile.

- Who are you unwilling to communicate with?

- Who is unwilling to communicate with you?

- Give a *good* reason for not communicating.

- Who is responsible for your communicating?

EVALUATING COMMUNICATION SKILLS

At times we need to evaluate our communication skills and measure our effectiveness for future growth.

- Place yourself on the following scales where you think these words describe the way you communicate with others:

    Rejecting _____ Accepting

    Critical _____ Nonjudgmental

    Hostile _____ Supportive

    Rebellious _____ Agreeable

    Distrustful _____ Trusting

    Disappointed _____ Considerate

    Resentful _____ Caring

    Unfriendly _____ Friendly

    Loner _____ Sociable

- Write down the names of three people whom you perceive as critical and judgmental.

- Write down the names of three people who are accepting and supportive.

- Write down the names of members of your family and place them on the preceding scales.

COMMUNICATING ACCEPTANCE

Becoming aware of our styles of communication can help us accept ourselves and others more fully.

- At times all of us perform such roles as helpers, advice-givers, agreers, and sympathizers—as well as analyzers, preachers, and judgers. Describe a situation where you used one of these roles. Describe a situation where someone else took one of these roles with you.

- Do you agree that we all make choices about wanting to be understood and about whether we are willing to risk self-disclosure?

- Are you willing to accept the limits another person sets on his or her privacy? What kind of a relationship can you have with this private person? Do you want such a relationship? How much time and energy are *you* willing to give?

- Describe a time when someone just listened to you. What did it feel like? Describe a time when you simply listened without trying to give advice, agree, or sympathize. How did the other person respond?

- Describe a time you said or did something that made someone feel really good.

- Describe a time someone else said something to you that made you feel really good.

- Compare the times of simply listening with the times of verbalizing acceptance. Which felt best to you?

The road sometimes doubles, to be sure, but . . . who can doubt that its general tendency is onward? To what goal we know not—it may be to some mountain where we shall touch the sky, it may be over precipices into the sea. But it goes forward. It is that thought that makes us strive to excel, each in his own way . . .

E. M. Forster

12

The Search for a Way of Life

This journal has presented concrete ways to explore some complex personal challenges. Because of multiplicity and change in individual lives however, neither simple nor complex theories offer permanent solutions to all problems. The individual search for a way of life leading to higher human possibilities continues until death. Since life and relationships can not be reduced to logic or science, ideas often contradict each other. Life is ambiguity, and each of us is in conflict with the givens of human existence.

Choose one of these human conditions to write about:

- Chronic dissatisfaction
- Vague feelings of emptiness
- An unwillingness to tolerate distress
- A yearning for a soulmate
- A longing to be loved

- Wanting to be connected to something larger than self
- Searching for meaning

In the future, review what you have written. Then write either on the same subject or on a new one.

Because the above human conditions never totally disappear, the greatest discovery we make is that we choose our inner attitudes which in turn can change the outer aspects of our lives. If you wanted to find stress, where would you look for it? *There is no stress in the world.* Stress is something we create inside of us. It is a product of how we perceive, define, and react to our world.

Our primary concerns in life are 1) death, 2) freedom, 3) isolation, and 4) meaninglessness. The ultimate battle in life is the war against death. Facing the knowledge that in the end we will lose the war, each of us has the power to create joy in living each day for whatever it has to offer with whatever meaning we create.

Death tells us we have no control over our mortality. Although humans spend much of their lives denying this reality, we must live with the fact that we will die, that our existence is transitory. We can however, choose from many kinds of existence. Once an individual assumes responsibility for his or her life, many possibilities appear.

Freedom tells us that we are free to choose and are ultimately responsible for our choices. We cannot live without making choices, yet we must live with the consequences of our decisions. We move through life with few absolutes, continually making new judgments and decisions as we go along, never knowing what the right decisions might be. We can not deny freedom by blaming something outside ourselves—other people, "luck", or "chance". We must consciously claim responsibility for our lives.

Isolation tells us that once we move out of the womb, each human body exists inside a single skin. Personal survival means each of us is threatened by the existence of other human beings whose central concern is also survival. We make peace pacts and social agreements to live together, then we deny that we are, in reality, isolated entities. We can choose however, to connect and commit ourselves to others in relationships.

Meaninglessness tells us that there are no absolute truths, that we can not find certainty, and that we create our personal reality. Each of us has the power of self-definition that comes through creating our own values. We explore certain ethical questions throughout our lives and freely choose unique and individual philosophical meanings for our lives.

Choose one of these topics and write down your response on a separate sheet of paper:

- I choose to value my anxiety which is an integral part of life.
- I choose to value my limitations. I am finite.

- I am an adult consciousness that exists alone. I choose to be independent and self-reliant, yet caring about others.
- I value differences because it tells me each of us is unique.
- I am able both to live and to reflect on my life.
- I always choose. Not to choose is also a choice.
- I can choose to love and care for others without expectations.
- My life is an endless process of growing and reaching out.
- My life includes inescapable ambiguities and contradictions that I experience as a result of the polarity of existence.
- I will *not* insist on certainty or being absolutely "right".
- My first and last choice is to say "yes" to life.

Return to these topics and develop them in depth whenever you experience distress or pain. They will lead you to your own truth.

Most of us want to live a "good" life, but we are troubled because we do not know what the expression "a good life" means or how to create it. The word "good" can be used as a moral judgment, or a persuasive statement of what we "ought" to do or be. "Good" can also be descriptive of certain socially-accepted behaviors. Value words are used to express tastes and preferences, to criticize and judge, to grade and evaluate, to advise and admonish, to persuade and dissuade, to praise and encourage. "Good" in the ethical sense is used as a description rather than a prescription and implies responsibility for personal decisions and choices.

We have learned to ask dependent, childlike questions that beg for some other source to take responsibility for giving meaning to life. Rephrase these by reclaiming your power as a responsible adult.

- If a thing is said to be good but no one can tell me what it is good for, how can I be expected to find it? Example:

  No one else can tell me how to live a "good" life. All the information I can find added to my own experiences will lead me to find my personal answers. I trust myself to find new answers as I change, learn more, and experience more of life.

- If no one can show me where the "good" is, how can it be reached?
- What must I do to live a "good life"? Good for what?

Because you are free and responsible, you create your own meaning.

Self-interest, physical survival, and protection of property are human drives. Society arises from a contract between individuals to advance self-interests but not to do so at the expense of others. Social values include the following:

1. The dignity and worth of the individual
2. Elimination of discrimination
3. Equality of opportunity

The ideal is that men and women of good will want a peaceful, prosperous world where education, reason, cooperation, and compassion bring about widespread happiness. But reality and experience teach us that most humans (including ourselves) will continue to act in their own best survival interests. We can strive for ideals and live with reality.

No one promised us a just, fair world. There is no Santa Claus to give us what we want. Every day bad things happen to good people. The young die tragically and freak accidents reach out at random to destroy good people in their prime. When forced to contend with suffering and tragedy, we are not alone. We can find a supportive group of others who have suffered the same tragedies—a life-threatening disease such as AIDS, cancer, Alzheimer's; the death of a child or spouse; the loss of body functions. A philosophical view can help us with problems of loneliness, moral confusion, and the pointlessness of life. An ethical commitment provides guidelines to enrich our daily lives.

Certain pursuits and conditions of life provide us with higher levels of satisfaction. Most of us feel happier when we are part of a group—family, neighborhood, company, church, or nation. We can give and receive support from others who also struggle with the pursuit of authentic meaning and human fulfillment.

ETHICAL DILEMMAS

Ethically, we believe that love, empathy, and understanding can solve some human problems. These ideal qualities are elusive and even saints can not apply them constantly and permanently to everyone unconditionally. As humans we have yet to evolve to greater heights of spirituality. We must live with opposites.

Make a list of diametrically opposed concepts:

- Justice denies mercy; and mercy denies justice
- Stability and change
- Tradition and innovation

- Public and private interests
- Order and freedom
- Growth and decay

With ethical problems, we must expect divergence.

Divergent problems cannot be solved in the sense of "formulas" or answers. They can, however, be transcended. Self-awareness plays a role. Love, compassion, understanding, and empathy become, at times, available as resources. Stronger, more intelligent people can use their superior qualities to transcend power through compassion. Once we are aware that opposites permeate everything we do (even though our logical mind rejects them) we can give up taking *positions,* trying to make our side right and the other wrong. Although opposites cannot be resolved, wisdom can sometimes reconcile needs. Human life depends upon mutually opposed activities. When we search for a new moral basis for society, a new foundation of ethics, we must contend with insoluble opposites. This wisdom leads us to develop our higher faculties and increase our human potential.

Personal Ethics

Ultimately the question of ethics is personal: "What can I do to live a worthwhile life?" Ethics, the discipline dealing with what is good and bad, offers opportunities for values to guide our choices and actions. To live, we must value life. Write on these personal concerns:

Physical care: a nutritious, balanced diet, regular exercise, freedom from disease and addictions (such as cigarettes, alcohol, drugs, sex), a clean environment (air and water), and the availability of medical care.

Emotional health: a positive attitude, a sense of humor, an ability to relax and balance stress, a capacity to experience delight and enjoyment.

Social support: mutual caring of family and friends, making social and community contributions, being a part of a group.

Spiritual enrichment: a positive outlook on life, a sense of personal worth, a productive life, a strong will to live.

An individual ethical system contributes to a sense of personal worth and well-being.

Productivity gives our lives personal meaning. The ideal, then, is to make our lives conform to the surest knowledge of those conditions that lead to human happiness and less personal unhappiness—for the good of mankind.

One basic struggle is between serving self-interests or the interests of others. Ethical questions are endless, the answers *always* debatable. No "right" answers exist.

Self-sacrifice seldom fulfills the self or others. The goal lies in the ethical process—the challenges of finding an acceptable ethical view without locking into an ethical position.

Consider these ethical questions without taking a position:

- Is lying always wrong—even if it protects another person?
- Is it ever acceptable to lie at work? At home? To friends?
- Have you taken sick days off from school or work when you were tired but were actually well enough to go?
- Have you exaggerated expenses or padded bills you have presented to others because you did an exceptional job?
- Have you tried to save money on your tax returns by padding deductions or not reporting income because you believe it is wrong to confiscate money from hard working people to support alcoholics, drug addicts, street people, military spending or some other government subsidized program you oppose?
- Would you be sexually unfaithful to a loved one who was physically or emotionally unable or unwilling to engage in sex?
- Have you used supplies at work or school for personal use?
- Do you make toll calls on phones that belong to other people?
- Have you picked up or used something that didn't belong to you?
- How many times have you copied answers on exams or gotten help on written assignments so that you could get a better grade? (Or fudged a point or two in games or sports so you would win?)

Rationalizations and justifications for our own behavior while judging other people's ethical behavior is common.

Guilt tells us we should have acted otherwise. Choosing the self over another leads to guilt. Mothers and fathers who work often feel guilty about leaving a child. If we believe self-interest is wrong, we experience guilt.

If we believe in putting others before our own best interests, we experience resentment. When we give up things we want or give time and energy to others, we want appreciation, love and recognition for our self-sacrifices. We often experience resentment and disappointment when we are not appreciated. The paradox is that others feel guilty when we sacrifice ourselves. Their guilt often turns to rejection of givers. Guilt or resentment often accompany choices.

Begin a journal of "self versus other" conflicts:

- Record times when you experience guilt
- Record times you experience resentment
- Explore feelings of ambivalence connected with giving to and receiving from others—gifts, money, or time

Ambivalence, contradictory thoughts, interpersonal conflicts, and social confusion can not be eliminated. They will always exist.

We can enrich our lives by transcending conflicts and dualities. If we lie or steal however, we challenge something basic in our own nature which threatens our self-image. In declaring war on another person for example, we declare war with our own concepts of decency. Painful experiences of resentment and guilt can lead to greater self-acceptance and wisdom when they are acknowledged.

Agreements

Agreements offer a group safety, predictability, security from chaos, a feeling of belonging and identity, economic security, and political order. Sometimes social agreements serve the society as a whole at the expense of the individual. As adults we eventually come to the conclusion that each of us is responsible for those agreements.

Agreements are not absolute. Like contracts, agreements have implied limits either in time or performance. In a whole system of agreements, many become outdated and must be revised. Only an immature child cries: "But you promised . . . you promised." People and situations change. When the government changes tax laws, previous agreements about "write-offs" no longer apply. When we find, as a nation or a state or a school district, that we have run out of money, past "promises" not to raise taxes or cut revenues must be revised. Insisting that politicians keep campaign "promises" is childish if new information proves those promises can not work. On a personal level, legal contracts such as marriage and business partnerships can be ended when they prove destructive. We can choose to reassess agreements.

The word promise *is a declaration that gives the person to whom the promise is made grounds for expecting a certain performance.*

- Tell about a time when someone broke a promise. How did you feel then? How do you feel now?

- Tell about a time when you broke a promise. How did you feel about breaking your promise? What reasons, defenses, justifications did you give?

- Are there differences between agreements and promises? Do you use words like "broken" when an agreement is revised?

- What do you want to do with promises, agreements, and expectations that no longer work?

We can rebel against, resist, ignore, or break an agreement. We can blame others for not keeping agreements. We can talk about why an agreement is not working. We can change agreements and end relationships. We can continue an agreement—stay married even if it is against our own or a spouse's best interests, stay on a job we hate even if it affects our health, continue some contract that is destructive out of a misguided belief that we are being loyal. Keeping destructive promises or agreements may come from fear of change or a lack of self-esteem.

We can choose to see agreements *not* as someone else's rules but as agreements with ourselves. We can acknowledge that we are responsible for our own agreements:

I can choose to end my agreements by quitting a job, dropping a class, getting a divorce. I am responsible. My agreements belong to me. When I keep my agreements, I am in control of my own life and "my life works". When I recognize that an agreement no longer works, I want to take responsibility for ending it, changing or replacing it; or simply handling it without guilt, excuses, rationalizations, or defensiveness.

ETHICS AND CHOICE

Life is *not* about being happy or successful—the choice is between existence and nonexistence. Life gives us the choice to exist in spite of existential problems. Life requires that we create and constantly recreate a personal reality. It is possible to transform our attitudes, to create and sustain the possibilities of life.

Through knowing about yourself, others, and life—about what is important at any given moment—you will continue to search, create, and recreate personal meaning. The statement required is: "I want to live." Once you have made that statement, then you can move to the pursuit of happiness and an ethical life.

You will be searching for ethical answers as long as you live. Remember . . .

1. You choose your state of mind.
2. You choose your attitudes toward life.
3. You choose your emotions.
4. You create your own self-image.

Answers are seldom final and never absolute. Every choice has its positives and negatives along with different consequences.

Choosing a World View

> *My life belongs to the whole community and as long as I live it is my privilege to do for it whatever I can.*
>
> *George Bernard Shaw*

Social scientists tell us every human being needs to be part of something larger than the self. To belong and be needed creates a basis for self-esteem and gives value to life. In addition to family, friends, and work, we belong to a community. Each of us can develop social responsibility and an ethical framework for making our contributions to the world.

Contentment, an internal state, is created by the wise, spiritually-developed individual who is often an ordinary person, unnoticed by others. This individual seldom needs approval, is not easily flattered, and often lives a simple life. Outward aims take second place to the inner life. In the end, fame is a delusion and wealth a mirage. A philosophical statement of personal values leads to creating personal meaning.

> *I want to have the moral strength to stand alone when necessary—that is, to go against the crowd if I feel that the crowd is doing something destructive. This means I will have the capacity to value integrity over popularity, decency over financial success. I want to develop a core of strength, a code of fairness and compassion for others; a faith and trust in my own feelings and values.*

Begin to form in your mind a philosophical statement.

- Sometimes such a statement comes by defining a single word—integrity, for example.

- It must be followed by specific examples of how your word gets manifested in behavior.
- Keep a record of times you act out your concept.

You will create your concept of a philosophical statement over time. Take notes and let your ideas form.

Integrity

Integrity is a state of being whole, entire, or undiminished. Integrity means being true to one's principles and to one's self. Integrity is manifested in doing what we say we will do, in not violating our ideals, in completing our work and our commitments. Although no one can live a life of total integrity, such a value provides a worthy goal. Integrity can transform a person, a relationship, a family, an institution, a country, and the world. Ethics enters our relationships when we directly or indirectly refrain from using persuasion or power to influence others in such a way as to interfere with their freedom of choice.

I will fight my human tendency to dominate, force, persuade or urge others to do what I want them to do. I will eliminate my use of moral language—good/bad, right/wrong, should/shouldn't—to manipulate others through attacking conscience. I will avoid exploiting, manipulating, and dominating others by allowing them to reclaim their power through self-assertion.

Equity of power results in cooperative efforts. The ultimate punishment for insisting on controlling others is self-destruction and the destruction of the relationship. The reward for allowing others to be free of your demands is *integrity*.

COMMON GROUND

If we search, we can find a core of cultural values and expectations that is shared worldwide—a timeless, global ethic that provides a common ground for all mankind. Make a list of mankind's shared values:

Justice: fair play

Liberty: degrees of freedom and the abolition of excessive constraints placed on individuals by others

Dignity: every human has an individual spirit and when we demean or belittle another person, we demean ourselves

Tolerance: recognition that each human must choose his values, that we must not force our ethics or religions on others

These, among others, are a few of the world's shared ethics.

The fact that we do not always act in accord with our ethics does not negate their value. Much of the time, we act out love in families, we work together on jobs, we volunteer to care for others in our communities. Most of the time, we obey the laws and respect the rights of others. We are learning to respect the beliefs and values of other cultures and that diversity and differences can be honored without danger. We recognize that communities are heterogeneous and pluralistic; a diversity of religious and ethnic differences. Cynicism or skepticism stems from fear of disappointment and destroys the possibilities of a "good" life. When we believe in the beneficence of the universe, we allow good things to happen.

Visualize the world of your dreams.

- Spend time thinking about what it would be like to live and move in your "good" world.

- Visualize the kind of people who are in that world . . . how they act . . . what you will do there . . . who you will care about . . . the costs and rewards of that life.

- Imagine your dream world until it feels as real as you can possibly make it. Then explore it, elaborate on it, and refine it before you initiate activities that lead to it.

This exercise can be continued as long as you live.

The shape of life is *not* like an arrow flying toward a target or a single trajectory toward a known goal. Composing a life has many beginnings and endings. It includes continuously redefining goals and using intellectual flexibility and creativity when changes, like a death or divorce, are forced upon us. Each interruption makes life a work of art, without perfect order or coherence, an improvisation composed from many diverse elements. Your life is your work of art!

CREATING A HOME

Each of us must create a personal point of view from which to function. Each of us needs a feeling of balance, a center of gravity on what might otherwise seem like the seesaw of life. Although this book has suggested many concepts for you to think about, many activities and experiences for bringing communication to consciousness, many suggestions about being responsible in the creating of meaning in your life, the ultimate personal project is for you to put together all this information and experience into some unique pattern—into a unified structure that is truly your own.

Philosopher Peter Koestenbaum suggests that each of us build a structure like a home: a shelter, a dwelling place, a retreat where the body/mind/heart is centered. From this center, you can move out into the world, explore, and experience all the facets of things, ideas, and people—knowing that you can always go home to find the energy, the strength, or the tranquility needed for life. In this central place so uniquely your own, you can pursue your ongoing search for authentic meaning and human fulfillment.

Communicating, the creating of personal meaning, builds this home: an internal reality out of which an authentic life can be lived. At any given moment this home can tell you who you are, give you identity, give you individuality. It can determine your values, describe your roles in life, and answer your questions. As carefully as you can, try to describe what this home means to you. In your imagery, it can have a physical reality in a forest, by a stream, high on a mountain, overlooking the sea, or simply in a quiet meadow. You can create any structure or form you wish in your imagination. Each day you can recreate Your Place.

THE JOURNEY

Traveling our personal journey can be elusive, costly, and at times out of control. Our personal projections into the future are speculations about ourselves over which we have some influence. The excitement and the disappointment, the hopes and rewards, are all part of what our existence is all about. Each of us must decide for ourselves as we create our individual lives. Philosophically it is possible to believe that you will make the best decisions for yourself given the person that you are at any particular moment in your life in the unique situation you might be in.

All questions, all ventures into thought, will vary from person to person. Yet they are worth exploring in written form here in your journal for, ultimately, understanding is necessary to human survival. Each of us is in the process of creating our lives. Our inner lives are beyond the biological limitations of the physical body. The inner journey, which you can record here on paper, can be touched with the hope of some triumph beyond mortal limits. We are endowed with wisdom that can lead us beyond the finite moment, beyond present time. Infinite love can be experienced in a finite moment. Inner freedom can be achieved, at moments, within a framework of outer limits. One of humanity's greatest feats has been the triumph of the inner life over exterior nature. We exist magically within individual bodies that can create dreams which transcend time. Only when we have ventured on our interior journey can we add our individual wisdom to mankind.